Clever as Serpents

Business Ethics and Office Politics

Jim Grote

and

John McGeeney

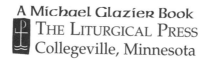
A Michael Glazier Book
THE LITURGICAL PRESS
Collegeville, Minnesota

Cover design by Greg Becker.

A Michael Glazier Book published by The Liturgical Press.

1   2   3   4   5   6   7   8   9

Library of Congress Cataloging-in-Publication Data

Grote, Jim, 1953–
    Clever as serpents : business ethics and office politics / Jim
Grote and John McGeeney.
        p.   cm.
    "A Michael Glazier book."
    Includes bibliographical references and index.
    ISBN 0-8146-5867-9
    1. Business—Religious aspects—Christianity.   2. Business ethics.
3. Work environment.   I. McGeeney, John, 1956–   . II. Title.
HF5388.G76   1997
174'.4—dc21   97-36164
                                                                      CIP

To my wife, Sissy, and my parents, Jim and Mary Jo, who introduced me to the puzzling oxymoron of the family business.

J. G.

To Linda.

J. M.

Remember, I am sending you out as sheep among wolves; so be clever as serpents and yet as simple as doves.

Matthew 10:16

The master praised the dishonest steward for his astuteness. For the children of this world are more astute in dealing with their own kind than are the children of the light.

Luke 16:8

Who is the rich man? He who is satisfied with what he has.

The Talmud

Contents

The authors' creative rendering of the theories of René Girard provides a perspective on the business world not attempted before. Despite the uniqueness of the argument, the book is easy to read and unusually accessible to a wide variety of people. It is appropriate for business ethics classes as well as adult education or management seminars.

Rev. John Haughey
Professor of Christian Ethics
Loyola University, Chicago

Clever as Serpents presents a spiritual, yet worldly, approach to the challenge of ethical conduct in organizations. The discussion is a readable, stimulating and refreshingly different approach to the subject of business ethics and management theory. Many practical suggestions are offered for anyone seeking a faith based approach to survival in the secular world of corporate America.

Ken Mudd
Senior Corporate Attorney
Louisville Gas & Electric

The complete text of *Clever as Serpents* was extremely interesting. Not only was it easy to read and well written, but the last five chapters were relevant and lifelike. I would recommend this book to anyone wanting to major in business or start their own company.

Karen Bell
Office Manager
Criminal Paralegal

I have read several self-help management books. These did not tap into my personal experiences. The information in *Clever as Serpents* has truly helped me think about my role in business and how I am affected by what goes on everyday. I am going to remember that success is getting what I want and not chasing what others want.

Teresa Sims
Aircraft Materials Supervisor
United Parcel Service

Clever as Serpents is a guide not only to ethical practices but for me a guide to sanity in a fast paced, highly competitive environment. The entire book has been an eye opener for me, in taking a look at business ethics from a spiritual standpoint.

Pat Wilson
Business Ethics Student

Acknowledgements

First and foremost, we want to thank our broker, Michael Downey, *sine qua non*. He has been an inspiration to our efforts, a pleasure to do business with, and a model of generosity for us to follow.

Our intellectual debt to René Girard is immense. Without his insights we would not have been able to make sense of the business world.

We are also grateful to Tim Fout for field testing this book in his business ethics classes.

And to the following people for taking their time and expertise to critique earlier drafts of this manuscript: Perry Bramlett, Jack Ford, Edward Freeman, Mary Jo Grote, Phil Hanson (¿Phil, dónde estás?), John Haughey, Susan Hickenlooper, Charles Mabee, Jim McWilliam, Carl Mitcham, Ken Mudd, J. J. Pakenham, Jerry Powers, Joe Rankin, John Rounds, Ellen Rudd, Patrice Tuohy, and James Williams.

Special thanks to Rosemary Smith for sharing her theory of "backseat driving" with us.

Finally to our children, Rachel, Catherine, Mark, Daniel, Teresa, and Sarah, and to our wives, for humoring us.

PART ONE

Theory

CHAPTER 1

Introduction

Human beings are rational animals.

Aristotle

People are idiots.

Dilbert

RATIONAL ANIMALS?

Office Politics: Is your boss unpredictable and intimidating? Are your subordinates high maintenance, whiny, and jealous? Are your peers always trying to do your job instead of their own? Are your customers fickle and demanding? Have you hit a glass ceiling? Are you stuck in a rut? Are your competitors stealing your best ideas before you can make money on them? Is your position being reengineered, downsized, rightsized, or outsourced? Are you overworked and underpaid? Are you drowning in office politics? If you can answer yes to any of these questions, then this book may be of interest to you. Unlike traditional academic approaches, we believe that a street smart business ethics must concern itself with these daily aggravations. How can you interact shrewdly with other people and current market conditions while staying true to your values?

Irrational Self-Interest: Because of the moral crisis in society today, there has been a resurgence of interest in the topic of ethics and virtue, particularly in the area of business ethics. Business schools throughout the United States are mandating courses in business ethics. Rather than reviewing the extensive literature on this subject, we have explored a more practical approach. Prevailing philosophical analyses into ethical questions are often based on abstract notions such as utility, equity, or liberty. Important as these analyses are, they share one common deficiency. They all presume the individual's ability to rationally calculate his or her own self-interest. We question this assumption. Experience shows that people are routinely, sometimes passionately, irrational in defining and pursuing their own "self-interest." The simple phenomenon of "buyer's remorse" reveals that self-interest is often fickle and fleeting.

Dilbert's Management Theory: One of the great management gurus of our time, Scott Adams, the creator of the cartoon character Dilbert, has arrived at a simple conclusion regarding the bizarre nature of human behavior in the workplace. He puts his theory elegantly and succinctly: "people are idiots."[1] Such brilliant insight should require little commentary. However, even Adams admits that his theory requires a corollary. According to Adams, most of us suffer from the nagging tendency to exempt ourselves from the above theory while still expecting others to behave rationally. "Surely not *moi?*" Economists and business theorists especially tend to be outraged or perplexed by irrational market behavior. Yet such behavior is often the norm. To quote Adams again: "we expect others to act rationally even though we are irrational."[2] But why are we outraged when Dilbert's principle is confirmed? Obviously, if people are irrational, there cannot be a rational answer to this question. The question merely confirms the corollary. Fortunately, Adams does not leave us in a total quandary. He proposes a cure of sorts to fit his negative diagnosis of the human condition. He argues that if we can come to peace with the fact that "people are idiots" and quit expecting rational behavior from them, then much of the tension in our lives will dissipate and we will be happier.

Aristotle's Ethics: Aristotle, the first Western philosopher of ethics, takes an entirely different approach than our consummate corporate cynic, Dilbert. Since Aristotle lived almost twenty-five centuries ago, he had little first-hand knowledge of the modern corporation. But he was a shrewd judge of character and spent plenty of time observing the vagaries of human behavior. Despite a lifetime embroiled in the politics of ancient Athens, he still concluded that human beings are rational animals.[3] Furthermore, he declared that the entire purpose of ethics is the rational quest for happiness. While most people agree that happiness is the goal of life, few of them agree on what happiness is or how it can be achieved. Some people argue that money leads to happiness. Others argue for sex. Still others argue for political power. And many people argue that ultimately only God can make us happy. The arguments have not changed much since the days of Aristotle. Whose advice do we follow, Aristotle's or Dilbert's? Or to put the question in the contemporary idiom of Dilbert, "how do idiots achieve happiness?"

Method in the Madness: While the business world can be an insane environment, we do not share Dilbert's cynicism completely. Although people may be irrational, there is a method to their madness. There is a reason for their irrational behavior. Understanding the method is one way out of the madness. In the words of one corporate attorney we consulted: "Once I learned how to detach from office politics and the corporate ladder, I became much more content and much less frustrated at work." We would like to share this contentment with you by exploring the method in the madness.

Experimental Ethics: Our analysis is not as simple as reading Dilbert (although Dilbert is a great place to start). Achieving happiness, as Aristotle first observed, is hard work. While the goal of this book is practical—finding happiness on the job— the means to that end entails thinking, and thinking is almost always painful. No pain . . . no gain. Please bear with us. This book is an experiment in business ethics. The approach is experimental because we are introducing working hypotheses, not established laws. Our experiment depends on you, the reader, and your observations of the business world. You are the subject of this experiment. Your experience furnishes the data on which to test these hypotheses. You are also the conductor of this experiment to the degree that you draw your own conclusions from them. Like you, we have shared this dual role of researcher and guinea pig. Our approach is designed to tap into the wisdom of your own experience and your own "war stories." In his search for truth, George Fox, the founder of the Quakers, despaired of finding any experts who could speak to his personal condition. (This was before the days of management theory and self-help books.) It was when he had no one to rely on but himself that he had his great spiritual awakening. His record of this insight in his *Journal* is instructive. In true Quaker fashion he sums up his insight simply: "This I knew experimentally."[4] If the hypotheses put forward in this book speak to your personal condition, you also will know they are true—experimentally.

Micro Business Ethics: This approach falls within the category of what Robert Solomon calls "micro business ethics," that is, "the concepts and values that define individual responsibilities and role behavior as opposed to the already well-developed theories of macro business ethics, the principles that govern or should govern our overall system of (re)distribution and reward."[5] Macro ethics has little direct effect on the average manager or office worker. "The ethical problems that the average manager faces on the job are personnel and routine administrative decision-making problems, not policy problems."[6] Our concern is with hands-on managers and workers, not policy wonks and academics. While appreciating the insights of macro systems like utilitarianism, social contract theory, entitlement theory, and Marxism, we remain unconvinced that these theories are useful to the issue of happiness and character. Aristotle reminds us repeatedly that in ethics, theory must always be subordinate to practice.[7] The fundamental issue in business is not utility or equity or liberty, but character. Stephen Covey has taken an important step in this direction with his criticism of the Personality Ethic of positive thinking in favor of the old fashioned Character Ethic of good habits, e.g. integrity, moderation, and industry.[8]

BUSINESS AS A RELIGIOUS ENTERPRISE

The Protestant Work Ethic: Furthermore, we interpret business as a religious enterprise. Modern capitalism is as much a religious as an economic phenomenon. Max Weber first popularized this insight in his brilliant study of the psychological conditions that make capitalist society possible. In *The Protestant Ethic and the Spirit of Capitalism,* Weber argued that the religious anxiety created by Calvin's doctrine of predestination led to an "ascetic compulsion to save" by Christian believers in their relentless search to find a sign of God's favor.[9] They saw material blessings as one of those signs. Weber termed this compulsion "worldly asceticism." Like Weber, we propose a theory of worldly asceticism, but one with different connotations.

Contra Weber: The religious roots of modern business culture are far older than the Calvinist milieu that Weber analyzed. The Protestant work ethic is merely one point on a spectrum of religious/economic cultures that extend back to primitive, tribal cults. Both office politics and financial markets often bear more resemblance to primitive, tribal behavior than to the sanitized Protestant work ethic. A purely philosophical analysis of religious behavior cannot be fruitful. Only a religious analysis of a religious enterprise will yield results. Given that we view business as a religious enterprise, it only makes sense that we analyze it from a religious standpoint.

Theoretical Hypotheses: We propose three working hypotheses about the modern marketplace.

1. The economic phenomenon of competition resembles the religious phenomena of idolatry (i.e. the mythic quest).

2. The behavior of both financial markets and office politics exhibits parallels to primitive sacrificial rites.

3. Both of the above phenomena are related to what we call the Management Complex. Like the Oedipus Complex, the Management Complex describes the human ambivalence towards authority figures.

These hypotheses will be explored in the first part of the book. They will provide a framework from which to build a practical ethics.

Practical Ethics: The practical ethics will be examined in the second half of the book. Since business is described as a religious phenomenon in part one, the ethics in part two follows from this insight. We propose a business ethics derived from the ancient monastic approach to truth, i.e. ascetic discipline. This approach is both practical and experimental. The *American Heritage Dictionary* defines an ascetic as "a person who renounces the comforts of society and leads a life of austere self-discipline." In the business world an ascetic is not a person who leaves the world to live in a monastery, but a person who accepts the discomforts of society in order to lead a life of austere self-discipline. This approach is not meant to denigrate monasteries. However, any monk who has led the monastic life for long will tell you that the hardest part of being a monk is not the physical hardships—manual labor, rising at 3:00 a.m., being a vegetarian, etc. The most difficult part is "life in community," putting up with the quirks of other people— office politics. Indeed the focused pursuit of any vocation requires a highly disciplined approach to discovering your personal niche within a community, whether that community be monastic, corporate, or otherwise.

Business Asceticism: Certain ascetic traditions in early monasticism sought to liberate the soul from the body, going to the extremes of promoting gruesome forms of "mortification of the flesh." Modern monasticism focuses on liberating the true self from the false self (cf. the writings of Thomas Merton). Business or "office asceticism" has similarly evolved from a simple ethic of hard work (the Protestant work ethic) to a more complex ethic of strategic focus. Contemporary business asceticism seeks to liberate the productive self from the competitive self. The word asceticism ultimately comes from the Greek word, *askesis,* a word that does not have anything to do with separating the body from the soul. *Askesis* simply means "exercise or training" (Liddell & Scott). It refers to a person who practices any art or trade, with the connotation of that person being industrious or athletic. *Clever as Serpents* is a training manual in the theory and practice of productive *and* ethical business practice. The modern office environment holds as much opportunity for spiritual and ethical development as the monastery.

Business Mythology: Within this framework, we hope to provide better techniques for survival in the marketplace, success in the marketplace, and service in the marketplace. However, the marketplace can only be seen for what it is after an exploration of those myths about the marketplace that conceal and reveal its true operations. Only by seeing clearly can we value proper choices; only through ascetic detachment can we see clearly. If our approach appears too cynical at times, it is because we want to ground our ethics in the harshness of the "real world." Hence our affinity with an ethics of asceticism. However, the real world need not be so harsh. True ethics should lead to hope and effective action. We all need to make money in order to live, preferably in ways that do not involve going to jail. But to have an ethics that is useful outside the classroom requires an analysis that is street smart. The conflict in the business world reveals itself in the metaphors we use to talk about the marketplace.[10]

The Market as Jungle: Upton Sinclair popularized the idea of the market as jungle in his investigation of the meat-packing industry in Chicago at the turn of the century. Most of us feel some affinity to the metaphor even if not in quite so grotesque a manner as described in *The Jungle*. Further, this metaphor of jungle applies to most work environments not traditionally associated with the business world. The jungle includes government bureaucracies, school systems, military machines, and even charity councils and church hierarchies. We focus on the business world, but the principles discussed here could be applied elsewhere.

The Market as Shark-Infested Waters: The marketplace is also often compared to shark-infested waters. Primers abound teaching novices how to swim with sharks. We are counseled that sharks are never docile in the presence of blood, but

CALVIN AND HOBBES © Watterson. Dist. by UNIVERSAL PRESS SYNDICATE. Reprinted with permission. All rights reserved.

instinctively join in the attack. The only way to swim with sharks is by prompt counter aggression, periodic anticipatory retaliation, and the encouragement of internal dissension among other sharks. "Those who cannot learn to control their bleeding," warns an anonymous bond trader, "should not attempt to swim with sharks, for the peril is too great."

No Ethics in Jungle or Ocean: Most managers and workers complain about unfairness in their work environment. What is amazing is that almost everyone accepts unfairness as a *sine qua non* for employment. From Machiavelli's *Prince* to the plethora of modern paperbacks explaining the secret of success, we are given plenty of advice on jungle warfare. Little has been written, however, on the structure of the jungle itself. How did the real world manage to become such an unpleasant place? What are the mechanisms that makes it tick? An understanding of these mechanisms will help us to survive, to succeed, and to serve others within the dynamism of the market.

Structure of the Text: Chapters 1 through 5 deal with a unique approach to management theory and the behavior of financial markets. We first examine the myths that hide the reality of the marketplace. Chapter 2 examines the myth of freedom; Chapter 3, the myth of competition. With the myths explored, Chapters 4 and 5 examine the secret of the marketplace through the theories of "borrowed desire" and the Management Complex. Chapters 6 through 10 propose practical techniques for dealing with the jungle of office politics. Chapter 6 applies the theory of "borrowed desire" to the dynamics of office gossip. Chapters 7 through 9 offer practical tips on survival, success, and service within the marketplace.

Notes

1. Scott Adams, *The Dilbert Principle* (New York: Harper Business, 1996) 2.

2. Ibid., 7.

3. Aristotle, *Nicomachean Ethics* I, 7.

4. Robert K. Greenleaf, *Servant Leadership* (New York: Paulist Press, 1977) 224.

5. Robert C. Solomon, *Ethics and Excellence* (New York: Oxford University Press, 1992) 110.

6. Ibid., 112.

7. Aristotle, op. cit., II, 2.

8. See Stephen Covey, *The Seven Habits of Highly Effective People: Restoring the Character Ethic* (New York: Simon & Schuster, 1989).

9. Max Weber, *The Protestant Ethic and the Spirit of Capitalism* (New York: Charles Scribner's Sons, 1958) 172.

10. For an expanded discussion of the role of metaphors in the business world, see Robert C. Solomon, op. cit., 22ff.

CHAPTER 2

The First Myth of the Market: Freedom

You'll excuse me, gentlemen. Your business is politics. Mine is running a saloon.

Humphrey Bogart, *Casablanca*

It is only under the shelter of the civil magistrate that the owner of valuable property can sleep a single night in security.

Adam Smith

RANDOM FAILURE AND THE BLAME GAME

New World Disorder: After the collapse of Communism and the end of the Cold War, the long expected world peace failed to materialize. Somehow the end of the ideological conflict has ushered in a regression to ethnic and racial warfare. Economic progress remains hobbled by cultural deterioration. While market economies have radically altered everyday life and improved standards of living at an unprecedented pace, violence and social anarchy are also on the rise. Witness recent events in Iraq, Somalia, Bosnia, Rwanda, Haiti, many of the former Russian satellites, as well as Los Angeles and Oklahoma City on the home front. Furthermore, the domestic economy has been characterized by economic anxiety, layoffs, downsizing, etc.

The Phenomenon of Random Failure: In the last couple of decades, we have seen social organizations of all kinds subjected to rapid and apparently random failure (e.g., the family unit, large nation-states, traditional U.S. corporations, mainstream religious denominations, the public school system, etc.). From the Communist Party's fall from dominance in Russia and Eastern Europe, to the end of IBM's dominance of the computer hardware market, to the utter collapse of civilized norms in Bosnia and Rwanda, unpredictable transformations of social behavior occur seemingly out of the blue. William Bennett has tracked the decline of U. S. society with his "Index of Leading Cultural Indicators."[1] For example, in the last thirty years teen suicide rates have tripled, illegitimate births have increased 400 percent, the divorce rate has increased 200 percent, violent crimes have increased 500 percent, and the child poverty rate has climbed to over 20 percent. However, while many explanations abound *after* the fact, accurate forecasting of these upheavals appears as rare an art as predicting the stock market.

Blame versus Explanation: Most "explanations" of random failures are veiled attempts to assign blame. Democrats tend to blame economics. Republicans tend to blame culture. Globally, the Communist system was "centrally planned," "corrupt," and "anti-capitalist," and thus inevitably failed. The Serbs, Moslems, and Croats in Bosnia are infected by "ethnic rivalry"; therefore they are at each other's throats. Nationally, homelessness and poverty are explained to be the inevitable results of the "welfare system" by the right or "racism" by the left. Far from explaining everything, these labels merely restate the problem in "acceptable" terms to the people who coin them. Blaming others creates a comfortable distance between failure and behavior. "We're not like them. It's not our fault!" Those who fail are those who deserve to fail.

Economic Explanations: For example, the centralized "big government" planning of Communist states has been a comfortable "explanation" for the total failure of these economies. But post-war Japan and Germany have become world class powers with carefully planned, centralized, and even corrupt industrial policies. The traditional debate between central planning and laissez-faire economics makes for good entertainment but for poor analysis. The basic relationship between government regulation and market activity is theoretically muddled. Both proponents and opponents of the free market are usually invested in a blame game that fails to illuminate this relationship.

FREE MARKET AS OXYMORON

The Problem of Free Markets: In the lean and mean 1990s, government regulation is routinely described as distortional, intrusive, or inefficient relative to various, otherwise "free" markets. Government should not interfere in the market decisions of individual actors precisely because each is freely choosing what he knows is best for himself. Regulation is inherently paternalistic and demeaning. Yet at the same time, government activity is what defines the property and contract rights that markets depend upon. Try walking into a supermarket tomorrow. Pick up a head of lettuce and smile at the store manager as you walk out the door without paying. In order to enforce the free marketplace, the manager will quickly call for government intervention. As you are being arrested, tell the police officer that it was your understanding that we had a "free" (equivocation intended) market in this country. Unless the government defines and defends the rights of private property, and punishes offenses against such rights as "crimes," a market cannot flourish.

Free Market and Law: The law defines markets. Should genes be patented? Should bank deposits be federally insured? Should manufacturers of faulty consumer products be subject to punitive damages? Should surrogate mothers' contracts be enforceable? Which drugs should be illegal? Should there be a legal market in pornography? Should lawyers advertise? Only government can answer these kinds of questions, yet the answers determine whether certain markets will be possible or not.

Surrogate Mother Contracts: Consider the enforcement by government of surrogate motherhood contracts. Will the courts forcibly transfer custody of a baby from the woman who bore the child to a couple who contracted for the child? Is the enforcement of this transfer merely an example of the "free market" or an act of government intervention into the spheres of personal liberty and privacy? (Or, is it government that creates and protects "privacy"?) Most courts hesitate to enforce such contracts and award custody based on the "best interests of the child," a traditional family law concept. Is this hesitancy less interventionist or more interventionist? The question is difficult because there is no "natural" marketplace in womb rentals.

Telecommunications Issues: As we write, Congress grapples with a major overhaul of the telecommunications industry. Telephone companies, cable companies, satellite companies, and consumer groups are all lobbying Congress intensely. Among recent proposals, an amendment has been offered that would ban obscene or indecent material on the Internet. A cultural battle is being waged between the original free-spirited "hackers," who oppose any government restraint on the exchange of ideas and information over the Internet, and the corporate "suits" who are trying to clean up the Internet by imposing sufficient standards to lure middle America into their Web. Frequently in such battles, something less than complete freedom is urged in order to assure the public of certain minimum standards of fairness, decorum, and safety so that the new marketplace will be a viable, profitable environment. Laws that regulate markets are often requested by the very people seeking to do business in those markets. Regulation helps launch infant industries. Entrepreneurs often demand government created incubators to protect their interests. Like beauty, regulation is in the eye of the beholder.

The Investment Industry: The investment industry is comprised of three major groups—banking, insurance, and securities firms—all clamoring for political favors. Tax-deferred insurance products exemplify a marketplace advantage created by the historical political clout of insurance companies and agents. Federally insured CDs are similarly maintained by the political clout of banks. Consider the example of the Savings and Loan crisis. In the early 1980s, the government raised FDIC insurance from $40,000 to $100,000 and allowed S&Ls to invest their government-insured deposits in riskier assets (like junk bonds or speculative real estate deals). Was this decision deregulation? Or was this another huge government subsidy of risky investments that distorted the market by making risky investments "artificially" more attractive? In hindsight, it looks far more like a massive subsidy than something so tame as the deregulation of a "government-shackled industry." High interest certificates of deposit, backed by the U.S. government, are less an example of a "free" market than a rigged one. The deregulation of the S&L industry left the taxpayers with approximately a $500 billion tab to pick up.

Ambiguity in Application: Government intervention is defined by social conventions that prescribe the limits and range of legislation. The combination, then, of politics and society determines the quality and quantity of market intervention. If you agree with other suppliers of video games that no game should be sold for under five dollars because such a move would trigger price wars and layoffs, you have committed a felony. If the government prosecutes you for this alleged offense, is this a governmental intervention or the natural working of a free market? If you sign a contract for the delivery of one hundred cases of beer by next Friday, make prepayment and fail to receive the goods on time, is the court order you obtain to return the money a government intervention or the natural working of a free market?

Public Policy or Free Market? Since all markets require enforcement of property and contract rights, there is no "natural" free market. Whether an industry in womb rentals exists or not depends on whether the government enforces womb rental contracts. Nevada, where prostitution is legal, will enforce a contract for sexual favors, but California will not. The macro rules of any market are necessarily determined by public policy. Rules insure sufficient order to allow for predictable trade, and once rules are ignored, confusion and conflict flourish. If you buy stock based on insider information, you can go to jail. Rather than a distortion of the free market, most of the securities industry believes that these rules are a protection that helps create a reliable market that small investors can trust. Securities law is the political triumph of one public policy preference over another. When product liability law took root, the free market in dangerous products was severely distorted. Law imposed an "artificial" value on safety features. Manufacturers of safe products were effectively subsidized because the rules were redefined in their favor. As a result of this legislation, awards for victims in product liability cases have soared, the most infamous being the punitive damages awarded to the woman who spilled McDonald's coffee on herself. Plaintiffs' lawyers seem to have temporarily gained control of this subsidy. However, being lawyers, their popularity as wealth recipients is not great, so the law will likely evolve again to combat such "abuses." Perhaps the ultimate market is simply "politics."

INVISIBLE HAND OR IRON FIST?

The Iron Fist: For Adam Smith, the market needed no government planning because it would be regulated as if by an "invisible hand." It is interesting to note that Adam Smith only mentions the invisible hand metaphor *once* in his massive tome, *The Wealth of Nations.*[2] Like the myth of the free market, the overplayed myth of the invisible hand hides the truth of the "iron fist" of governmental intervention and regulation. A totally unregulated market is no market at all. It is theft and war rather than commerce and trade. Capitalism could not emerge historically until the warrior mentality of feudal knights was replaced by the centralized government of nation-states. Witness the broad unwillingness of U.S. companies to invest in the Soviet Union after the collapse of Communism. There was not enough political stability (i.e., government intervention) to secure free trade. Unless there is a referee to enforce the rules of the game, there is no game.

The Failure of Communism: Markets, however, are not totally unfree. While there are no purely free markets, even rigged markets contain very different degrees of freedom. We are not engaging in an argument for Communism. The failures of Communism are obvious. Communist governments tend to operate inefficient, rigged markets that favor the Party elite and cheat the working class. Nor are we arguing that business needs more government regulation. The question is not the *quantity* of government regulation, but the *quality* of government regulation.

Government Largesse: One qualitative problem in capitalist democracies is that government intervention often favors big business over small business.

> [In the United States] the government has been used almost exclusively to the benefit of the equestrian classes—intervening in the steel industry, subsidizing American exporters through the Export-Import Bank, rescuing the Chrysler Corporation as well as hundreds of banks, guaranteeing farm prices and farm credit institutions, approving the inside trading preliminary to corporate mergers and takeovers, sustaining the defense industries and protecting the insurance companies.[3]

The small guy is not free to play directly in these games. Chrysler was bailed out by the U.S. government. Could the typical small manufacturer or corner hardware store get the same deal?

Republican Socialism: The acid-penned financial columnist, Michael Lewis, has nicknamed this phenomenon "Republican Socialism." Lewis goes so far as to argue that cutting the capital gains tax (anywhere below the highest marginal income tax rate) distorts the free market in investment capital by funneling capital investment into areas based solely on tax strategies.

> But as anyone knows who has gazed upon the empty skyscrapers thrown up during the mid-1980s construction boom, driven by real-estate tax breaks, all investment is not socially productive investment. There is no reason to believe that the quest for capital gains will be any less wasteful than other Government-induced economic behavior.[4]

Democratic Capitalism: This problem of veiled self-interest applies as much to Democrats as to Republicans, but in a different fashion. Republicans sometimes fail to see the iron fist of government lurking behind the invisible hand. Democrats sometimes fail to see the individual self-interest hidden behind political appeals to the common good. The government is not a disinterested umpire, but a very eager participant in markets. As Milton Friedman states:

> In the government sphere, as in the market, there seems to be an invisible hand, but it operates in precisely the opposite direction from Adam Smith's: an individual who intends to serve the public interest by fostering government intervention is "led by an invisible hand to promote" private interests, "which was no part of his intention."[5]

Liberal Democrats and conservative Republicans are quick to see the beam in their opponent's eye, but slow to see the mote in their own. As Bill Bradley stated regarding the fundamental contradiction in the Republican agenda: "The free market that economic conservatives champion undermines the moral character that social conservatives desire." However, Bradley fails to see that the same logic applies to the Democratic agenda: The regulated market that economic liberals champion undermines the moral freedom that social liberals desire. Democrats offer a contradictory mixture of economic regulation and laissez-faire morality. Republicans offer a contradictory mixture of moral regulation and laissez-faire economics.

In Summary: Markets require rules, and rules require enforcement by some referee. The difference between a constructive referee and a tyrannical dictator may be drastic, but it is not the difference between intervention and non-intervention. While the government must act as a referee in markets, we can never conclude that it is neutral about those markets. It is always subject to influence by the players. The shrewd entrepreneur realizes the importance of taking his congressional representative out to dinner once in a while. To the extent that government is lobbied by special interest groups, it is part of the market.

Economics and Politics: Economics is always a function of politics. To think otherwise is to enter the realm of mythology. The myth of the free market masks the power of special interests, whether the interests of organized labor, of the *Fortune 500,* of the media or of the government itself. From farm subsidies to minimum wage laws, from federal deposit insurance to federal patent approvals, the necessary evil of government regulation always tips the scales in someone's favor at someone else's expense. The myths of the free market and the invisible hand are a slick cover for the less than subtle ways that the referee allocates success and failure to the players.

Notes

1. William J. Bennet, *The Index of Leading Cultural Indicators,* vol. 1 (Washington, D.C.: The Heritage Foundation, 1993).

2. Robert C. Solomon, *Ethics and Excellence* (New York: Oxford University Press, 1992) 86.

3. Lewis Lapham, *Money and Class in America: Notes and Observations on Our Civil Religion* (New York: Weidenfeld & Nicolson, 1988) 135.

4. Michael Lewis, "Republican Socialism," *The New York Times Magazine* (November 26, 1995) 32.

5. Milton and Rose Friedman, *Free to Choose* (New York: Harcourt Brace Jovanovich, 1980) 5–6.

CHAPTER 3

The Second Myth of the Market: Competition

The amassing of wealth is one of the worst species of idolatry.

Andrew Carnegie

In any market, as in any poker game, there is a fool. . . . any player unaware of the fool in the market probably is the fool in the market.

Warren Buffett (c/o Michael Lewis)

THE PSYCHOLOGY OF COMPETITION

The History of Productivity: The other major myth of the market assumes that competition is a stimulus to productivity. The relationship between competition and productivity is ambivalent. While "controlled" competition may be a stimulus to production, the state of pure competition results in "the war of all against all" (Hobbes). Obviously this state is destructive rather than productive. The term "productivity" likewise is ambivalent. In the most primitive economy, productivity was measured by the rate of capture, the first law of the jungle. Wealth increased by capturing plants or animals (foraging and hunting), capturing people (slavery), or capturing others' property (conquest). As humankind progressed, agriculture replaced capture as the means of production. Productivity began to be measured by ownership of land, and landed aristocracies ruled the world for most of recorded history. The Industrial Revolution changed this benchmark of ownership, and capital replaced land as the primary means of production. Capital is production embodied in organic labor and machinery (i.e. dead labor).

The Future of Productivity: Francis Bacon wrote that "knowledge is power;" yet, now the converse of that statement is more accurate—"power is knowledge." Today productivity is moving beyond the realm of capture, agriculture, and capital to the realm of knowledge. Peter Drucker has documented this transition in his book, *Post-Capitalist Society.* This transformation from capital to knowledge is beyond the scope of this book. However, our argument arrives at conclusions similar to those of Drucker, only from a different angle. Both approaches question the myth that "competition spurs productivity."

Benchmarking as a Clue to the Market: The recent management tool of benchmarking clearly exemplifies the ambivalent nature of competition. Benchmarking offers a clue to what makes the market tick. Michael Spendolini defines benchmarking as a "continuous, systematic process for evaluating the products, services, and work processes of organizations that are recognized as representing the best practices for the purposes of organizational improvement."[1] Benchmarking entails researching and mimicking the practices of successful businesses. Benchmarking is a highly conceptual, systematic process. For example, AT&T has published a book of over one hundred pages as its internal twelve–step process for benchmarking.

The Contradiction of Innovative Imitation: However, the analytic process in benchmarking hides a darker, less rational side. The imitation of competitors can lead to sameness and conformity rather than to innovation and diversity. Benchmarking produces innovation only when the best practices of "non-competitors" are translated into new contexts. Corporate folklore has it that Domino's Pizza studied the package delivery techniques of Federal Express in redesigning its own pizza delivery services. On the other hand, much of what passes for benchmarking in Corporate America is the age-old obsession with the practices of one's direct competitors.

The Generic Manager: Benchmarking is precisely the kind of management fad promoted by politically astute executives who lack sufficient knowledge about the nuts and bolts of their particular business. The economist Robert Samuelson, has predicted the demise of the "generic manager," one who lacks knowledge of specific products. According to Samuelson, knowledge resulting from apprenticeship in a company is more important than an MBA. As Samuelson says:

> Roger Smith, GM's chairman between 1981 and 1990, exemplified this sort of know-nothing executive. When asked by *Fortune* to explain what went wrong, he answered: "I don't know. It's a mysterious thing." To fathom what went wrong, Smith truly had to understand how automobiles are designed and made; he apparently never did.[2]

Lee Iacocca makes a similar skeptical observation regarding generic management skills.

> I've never gone along with the idea that all business skills are interchangeable, that the president of Ford could be running any other large corporation just as well. To me, it's like the guy who plays saxophone in a band. One day the conductor says to him: "You're a good musician. Why don't you switch over to the piano?" He says: "Wait a minute. I've been playing the sax for twenty years! I don't know beans about the piano."[3]

Management know-how can never make up for a lack of product knowledge.

Competition and Idolatry: Productivity is ultimately rooted in human creativity. Competition, however, adversely affects creativity because of the mindless obsession it breeds among competitors. Competition replaces creativity with conformity and ultimately with idolatry. Idolatry did not go out of fashion with the Israelites worshipping the Golden Calf in the wilderness. Idolatry never goes out of fashion; an obsession with fashion is the heart of idolatry.

Idols of Silver and Gold: Consider Oliver Stone's modern morality play, *Wall Street*. The star of the movie is the ultra capitalist, Gordon Gekko (Michael Douglas). Who can forget his famous "greed is good" speech? Mr. Gekko clearly exhibits a competitive streak. Surrounded in his office by a bird's-eye view of New York City, a battery of computers, and an army of lawyers, Gekko does battle daily with a vast array of impersonal competitors, i.e. market forces. Only in the privacy of the steam room with his disciple, Bud Fox (Charlie Sheen), do we catch a glimpse of Gekko's real competitors: the well-born "Ivy League schmucks" who snubbed his earlier efforts to climb the ladder of success. His obsession with these schmucks leads to his downfall at the end of the drama. Herein lies the ambivalent nature of competition. Our competitors become our models, our benchmarks of success, our secretly worshipped idols. Our competitors represent the never quite fully attained image of success that we aspire to. The more we fight our competitors, the more we resemble them, and the less creative we are. As the ancient Psalm reminds us:

> Their idols are silver and gold,
> the work of human hands.
> They have mouths but they cannot speak,
> they have eyes but they cannot see,
> they have ears but they cannot hear,
> they have nostrils but they cannot smell.
> Their makers will come to be like them
> and so will all who trust in them. (Psalm 113)

Non-Productive Competition: Gekko's confession reveals the non-productive side of competition. Competition relates only tangentially to superior products and market share. The heart of competition is an obsession with the quirks and strategies of competitors rather than with the characteristics and desires of customers. Competition can be temporarily productive. In the short run, it may spur productivity by lighting a fire under management. In the long run, it destroys productivity because the focus on rivalry as an end in itself distracts management from the focus on the customer and on the product. As the battle becomes more important than the product, the virus of idolatry eats away at a company from the inside. Idolatry is the Pac-Man that destroys companies from within. In the business world, when apparent random failures occur, such as IBM and General Motors in the late 1980s, it is crucial to search out the virus of competition and see at what point it went over the edge and when paranoia replaced productivity as the *modus operandi* of the organization. Our study attempts to expose the mechanism that converts healthy competition into obsessive competition.

THE BIOLOGICAL METAPHOR OF COMPETITION

Nature as Competitive: Laissez-faire capitalism finds special justification in the biological theory of Darwin's "Survival of the Fittest." Charles Darwin's *The Origin of Species* (1859) argues that organic beings increase at a rate so great that the progeny of any single pair would crowd the earth if their multiplication were not held in check. Competition among species for survival provides this system of checks and balances that Darwin termed natural selection.

Social Darwinism: In the struggle for existence, competition results in the survival of the fittest. In economic terms, the rich are viewed as simply better adapted to the conditions of social life than are the poor. Those who wish to remove or mitigate competition go against the very laws of nature. Herbert Spencer, Thomas Huxley, and J. D. Rockefeller spread the doctrine of biological competition with great effectiveness. Thomas H. Huxley outlined this "beak and claw" nature in his 1888 essay "The Struggle for Existence in Human Society." It has become accepted wisdom in our culture that the marketplace, like the animal kingdom, continually evolves to a higher state through the natural process of competition.

Nature as Cooperative: But Darwin and Huxley are not the final word, even in the field of biology. Reciprocal altruism is a key force in the survival of the fittest. Actually this theory is not new. Peter Kropotkin was an early forerunner of this theory in his book *Mutual Aid* (1902). Kropotkin never denied the reality of struggle in existence; however, his zoological studies convinced him that the more animals cooperated, the better their chances for survival.

Wolves and Mutual Aid: Kropotkin argues that mutual aid rather than the struggle for existence is the fundamental advantage in the evolution of species.

> Sociability is as much a law of nature as mutual struggle. . . . Mutual aid favors the development of such habits and characters as insure the maintenance and further development of the species, together with the greatest amount of welfare and enjoyment of life for the individual, with the least waste of energy.[4]

The most aggressive of animals—the Siberian wolf, the jackal, lions, tigers, and leopards—illustrate associations of mutual aid. These animals cooperate with each other and hunt in packs.

The Elimination of Competition: Kropotkin claims that better conditions for survival are created by the elimination of competition—by means of mutual aid and mutual support rather than by practicing the rituals of competition. He summarizes: "In the great struggle for life—for the greatest possible fullness and intensity of life with least waste of energy—natural selection continually seeks out the ways precisely for avoiding competition as much as possible."[5] Citing hundreds of examples from the animal kingdom, Kropotkin shows how cooperation more efficiently insures survival than competition.

Kropotkin Updated: The contemporary scientist and author, Lewis Thomas, makes the same argument for mutual aid at the more minute level of bacteria. Thomas makes the case for the existence of genuine altruism among species of anaerobic bacteria. He summarizes his involved and technical argument:

> My argument, stated generally and briefly, is that the driving force in nature . . . is cooperation. In the competition for survival, natural selection tends, in the long run, to pick as real

> winners the individuals, and then the species, whose genes
> provide the most inventive and effective ways of getting along.
> The most inventive and novel of all schemes in nature, and per-
> haps the most significant in determining the great landmark
> events in evolution, is symbiosis, which is simply cooperative
> behavior carried to its extreme.[6]

Thomas admits that competition is often more advantageous
in the short-run, but never in the long-run.

Economic Inheritance: Perhaps the best argument against
social Darwinism comes from one of the world's most promi-
nent financiers, George Soros. Soros' argument avoids the com-
plexities of evolution and genetic inheritance. His is simply a
common sense observation about economic inheritance.

> The laissez-faire argument against income redistribution in-
> vokes the doctrine of the survival of the fittest. The argument is
> undercut by the fact that wealth is passed on by inheritance,
> and the second generation is rarely as fit as the first.[7]

If the ability to make or manage money is not an inherited
trait, why is the descent of wealth through families considered
"freer" or more competitive than the distribution of wealth by
government?

THE LOGIC OF COMPETITION

The Dilemma of Competition: Social Darwinism has also
been under attack from another discipline—computer science.
The philosopher and psychologist, Anatol Rapaport, developed a computer program called TIT FOR TAT which shows
that, over the long haul, cooperative strategies win out over
competitive strategies. His program tested and proved the
theory called the "Prisoner's Dilemma." The Prisoner's
Dilemma has been published in numerous versions, but the
basic outline is as follows.[8]

The Prisoner's Dilemma: Imagine two prisoners who have
been arrested for armed robbery. Both prisoners are inter-
rogated separately and have no opportunity to share their

respective strategies with each other. There are four possible scenarios related to their confessions.

1. If neither of the prisoners confesses, the prosecution's case against them will be weakened, and both will receive light sentences of three years in prison.

2. If both of the prisoners confess, they will receive harsh punishments, but less than the maximum.

3. If the first prisoner confesses and the second does not, the first prisoner will receive the lightest treatment of two years and the second prisoner will receive the harshest penalty of twelve years.

4. If the second prisoner confesses and the first does not, the second prisoner will receive the lightest treatment of two years and the first prisoner the harshest penalty of twelve years.

The schema for the dilemma looks like this:

Prisoner #1

		Confess	Don't Confess
Prisoner #2	Confess	9 years for both	12 years for **#1** 2 years for **#2**
	Don't Confess	2 years for **#1** 12 years for **#2**	3 years for both

Cooperation or Paranoia: If the prisoners were able to talk to each other, they would agree not to confess and both would receive light sentences (three years). Or, if the prisoners had an altruistic view of each other, they might similarly come to the same conclusion. But, if both prisoners are paranoid that the other will confess, they will react accordingly and will either both receive a harsh sentence (nine years), or one will receive the maximum sentence (twelve years). We conclude that competition and mistrust is not in the best interest of a group or of an individual in a group. The Prisoner's Dilemma shows that altruism can coincide with self-interest.

The Death of Competition: James Moore argues that modern firms have established fundamentally new business strategies based on mutual cooperation. Whole new packages of services beyond the capacity of any single company have created the ability to redefine market needs. "As Bill Joy of Sun Microsystems said so aptly, 'The goal is not to win at someone else's game, but rather to change the game to one that you can win.'"[9] Frequently, in order to change the game, an entire group of service providers must cooperate strategically in imagining, designing, and implementing their dominance of a brand new market. One classic example was the war between the VHS video tape format and Betamax. Ultimately VHS triumphed because the group of cooperating providers was broader than that of Betamax. The introduction of compact discs was similarly the result of a broad cooperative effort in the recording industry which required manufacturers of electronic equipment, distributors, and record companies to agree in advance upon technical standards and strategy.

Conclusion of Chapter 3:   Psychology, biology, and logic all pierce the myth that competition rather than cooperation leads to innovation and productivity. However, it is also clear that competition creates incentive. In order to understand the ambivalent nature of competition it is necessary to understand the secret of the market.

Notes

1. Michael Spendolini, *The Benchmarking Book* (New York: Amacom, 1992) 9.

2. Robert J. Samuelson, "The Death of Management," *Newsweek* (May 10, 1993) 55.

3. Lee Iacocca, *Iacocca: An Autobiography* (New York: Bantam Books, 1984) 141–2.

4. Peter Kropotkin, *Mutual Aid: A Factor in Evolution* (Boston, MA: Extending Horizons Books, nd.) 6.

5. Ibid., 74.

6. Lewis Thomas, *The Fragile Species* (New York: Charles Scribner's Sons, 1992) 139–40.

7. George Soros, "The Capitalist Threat," *Atlantic Monthly* 279, no. 2 (February 1997) 53.

8. For example, see Robert C. Solomon, *Above the Bottom Line: An Introduction to Business Ethics,* 2nd edition (New York: Harcourt Brace Jovanovich, 1994), pp. 151ff.

9. James Moore, *The Death of Competition: Leadership and Strategy in the Age of Business Ecosystems* (New York: Harper Business, 1996) 54.

CHAPTER 4

The Secret of the Market: Borrowed Desire

I wanna be like Mike.

T.V. ad with Michael Jordan

Man differs from other animals in his greater aptitude for imitation (mimesis).

Aristotle

The Structure of Desire

So Why Do We Compete? We have seen in the last two chapters that mythology runs rampant in our thinking about markets and competition. Competition is often self-destructive, even of its own professed goals. While competition can be effective in the short-run, its long-term consequences are problematic. Competition does not always spur productivity, but frequently becomes a distraction. An obsession with competitors leads to tunnel vision. Peripheral vision is necessary in order to be creative in the marketplace. So why do we persist in this competitive behavior? Economists assume that competition is fueled by the profit motive. But what motivates this relentless quest for profit? Conventional wisdom states that the market is moved by two factors: greed and fear. We add a third motive, pride, and propose three extreme models or caricatures of the desire for profit.

Profit and Greed: One motive is the insatiable drive for material goods. Madonna's "material girl" is the classic example of the consumer. For the material girl, sexuality is hardly the goal in life, but merely a powerful means for getting what she really wants: "more stuff!" In the material girl's image, greed is presented as the height of fashionable behavior. Gordon Gekko moralizes that greed is good. The material girl advertises that greed is hip. There is no question that greed is a major engine behind consumer behavior in the United States. Americans spend their discretionary income in almost humorous consumption patterns:[1]

$44 billion a year on soft drinks
$12 billion on candy
$29 billion on diets
$35 billion on sports activities
$2 billion on golf equipment
$5.5 billion on video games
$19.5 billion on lottery tickets
$8 billion on pets
$5 billion on new pools and accessories
$3.5 billion on women's sheer hosiery
$2.7 billion on skin care
$1.5 billion on fingernails

One and a half billion dollars on fingernails? No wonder the total spending in our country is referred to as the "Gross" National Product. However, this acquisitive behavior is not the only explanation for the profit motive. If everyone played the part of the pure consumer, the economy would suffer from lack of investment capital. Americans are accused of this vice all the time. Yet our mutual funds are full of billions of dollars that people have chosen not to spend on the immediate gratification of material goods. What motivates this delay in consumer gratification?

Profit and Fear: Another instructive extreme is Ebenezer Scrooge. If the desire for material goods is the engine of capitalism, how do we account for the miser? Perhaps profit also reflects a desire for financial security as well as for material goods. Ebenezer Scrooge saved almost everything he made and consumed almost nothing. He had consummate financial security but was completely unhappy. In fact the word "miser" is connected to the word miserable. The miser's effort to secure capital is inherently self-defeating because the more one acquires the more one needs to protect. While greed sells consumer goods, fear sells mutual funds and insurance products. We all fall prey to Ebenezer's paranoid caricature of thrift and asceticism where "time is money" and "a penny saved is a penny earned." Karl Marx gives a brilliant satire of the miser:

> The science of wealth is therefore simultaneously the science of renunciation . . . the science of asceticism . . . Self-renunciation, the renunciation of life and of all human needs, is its principal thesis. The less you eat, drink and buy books; the less you go to the theater, the dance hall, the public house; the less you think, love, theorize, sing, paint, fence, etc., the more you save—the greater becomes your treasure which neither moths nor rust will devour—your capital. The less you are, the less you express your own life, the more you have.[2]

The miser sacrifices his or her self for the sake of capital. However, if the consumer and the miser were the only models of capitalism, how do we account for the phenomenon of risk?

Profit and Pride: The third extreme is personified by Donald Trump. For the Donalds of the world, the art of the deal is more important than material goods or financial security. The gambler must risk everything, transcending greed and fear. A desire for self-aggrandizement drives this willingness to take risks. The venture capitalist seeks adventure as much as capital. Without pride, people would avoid market risk once they had amassed a certain amount of money. Yet how many billionaires think they have enough? They may be swimming in consumer goods and financial security, but other challenges gnaw at them, e.g., the challenge of being "number one." The gambling instinct is a crucial aspect that is often overlooked in analyzing the profit motive. For the shrewd players that have surpassed their base instincts of greed and fear, something more is required to keep them motivated. As Vince Lombardi said, "Winning isn't everything, it's the only thing." For the gambler, money is merely a social scorecard, a way of keeping track of who is winning and who is losing.

Profit and Motive: The consumer, the miser, the gambler . . . who makes the market tick? And, what is the downside to each extreme? The consumer suffers from buyer's remorse, the miser suffers from paranoia, and the gambler from hollow victories. Each of these archetypes helps to describe but does not fully explain the profit motive. We can inquire still further. Why are we greedy? Why are we afraid? Why are we proud? Or we can ask: is there a more satisfactory explanation that covers these three, sometimes contradictory, motives? Perhaps Max Weber was correct in arguing that a kind of religious passion lies behind the modern profit motive.

Profit and Idolatry: It is not natural for people to work as intensely as they do in capitalist societies. The medieval peasant or the noble savage preferred a life of ease and few material goods to a life of industry and a mountain of "stuff." As Weber says: "A man does not by nature wish to earn more and more money, but simply to live as he is accustomed to live and to earn as much as is necessary for that purpose."[3] If given a raise, a medieval peasant would be more inclined to work less than to spend more. According to Weber, the desire for profit is not a natural impulse, but betrays a religious passion. This passion does not originate with Calvinist anxiety, but is as old as humankind. The ancients referred to it as idolatry. It is not by accident that the first of the Ten Commandments is a condemnation of idolatry. All other transgressions follow from this fundamental transgression. The phenomenon of idolatry helps to explain the herd mentality and conformism of consumers, the asceticism and paranoia of misers, as well as the obsessive-compulsive streak of gamblers. In order to better understand the relationship of idolatry to the marketplace, it is necessary to step away from the business world and view it from the outside.

A New Theory of Human Behavior: One theory that explains marketplace behavior more profoundly than the above examples hails from an unlikely source—the theories of the contemporary French scholar, René Girard. Girard has articulated a concept that is revolutionizing the human sciences of economics, psychology, anthropology, and sociology. This concept is *mimesis* or imitation. Students of Girard have compared his analysis of mimesis in the human sciences to Newton's discovery of gravity in the physical sciences.

> Taking as a model the theory of universal gravitation in physics, let us propose the hypothesis that there is a single principle at the foundation of all the human sciences: *universal mimesis.* In both psychology and sociology, the most basic and elementary manifestation of this principle is the force of attraction that draws people together and determines their interest in one another. Should the science of psychology wish to pursue this analogy to physics, it could be said that the mimesis between two individuals is the force of attraction that each simultaneously exerts on the other and submits to. This force is proportional to the mass, as it were, of each and inversely proportional to the distance between them.[4]

This force of attraction and repulsion is rooted in the phenomenon of imitation. Girard refers to this phenomenon by many names—metaphysical desire, mimetic desire, triangular desire, secondhand desire. To show its affinity to the business world, we choose to describe it with a financial metaphor as "borrowed desire."

Desire and Adultery: The oddest fact about borrowed desire is its triangular structure. A classic example of borrowed desire is adultery. In *The Eternal Husband,* a short story by Dostoyevsky, the husband is a man fascinated (i.e., attracted *and* repelled) by his wife's lovers. The fact that other men desire his wife makes the wife more desirable in the husband's eyes. The desire of the lovers validates the desire of the husband; he borrows the desire of other men to reaffirm to himself that he made the right choice in marriage. At the same time, he obviously resents them. As the photographer, Richard Avedon, quips: "Three is never boring."

Desire and the Nursery: Another simple example of borrowed desire is from the nursery. "Place a certain number of identical toys in a room with the same number of children; there is every chance that the toys will not be distributed without quarrels."[5] (On occasion the same behavior may be observed in some groups of managers.) Observe small children with their older siblings and it becomes obvious that these little creatures are mimetic machines. At this stage of development, however, mimesis is an innocent, educational process. Adult mimesis, on the other hand, can be less innocuous. It can be summed up by the old cliche—"keeping up with the Joneses."

The Problem of Scarcity: Girard's analysis of borrowed desire relocates the central problem of economics. Classical economics focuses on increasing the amount of goods and services to the human community, i.e. the wealth of nations. There are not enough goods to go around. How can we produce more? Economics is typically defined as "the study of the allocation of scarce resources toward the satisfaction of human desires." For both Adam Smith and Karl Marx, scarcity is the fundamental economic problem. There are two solutions to the problem of scarcity—increase resources and/or reduce desires. Economists generally emphasize increasing resources. (One qualification to this assertion might be the Keynesian focus on *demand* management. However, even the Keynesians see the issue of demand as a means to an end—the end being an increase in the gross national product. Their emphasis is still on increasing the total supply of goods.) At the risk of over-simplification, we might conclude that economics focuses on the "resources" side of the equation and ethics on the "wants" or "desires" side of the equation. Both approaches can be considered equally pragmatic to the extent that they both "solve" the problem of scarcity.

The Problem of Fact and Value: Most economists assume that human desires are unlimited and that, in and of themselves, these desires are not a proper subject of scientific inquiry. Questioning the ethics of particular desires entails making value judgments that are not within the domain of scientifically verifiable facts. The investigation of desire *qua* desire is therefore abandoned. Granted, we cannot attain the same precision in ethics that we can in natural science; and economics models itself after natural science. However, the inability to attain strict precision in a given subject is not a legitimate reason to abandon the study of that subject. Such an attitude reflects a prejudice rather than a logical argument. As Aristotle reminds us, the educated person "searches for that degree of precision in each kind of study which the nature of the subject at hand admits."[6]

The Problem of Desire: For the sake of our experiment in ethics, let us assume that the fundamental economic problem is not scarcity, but desire itself. The problem of wanting precedes the problem of getting. If this is the case, an analysis of human desire should precede an analysis of the allocation of resources. George Bernard Shaw expresses the problem of desire succinctly: "There are two tragedies in life. One is not to get your heart's desire. The other is to get it."[7] Since none of us are certain about what will make us happy in life, we constantly experiment with our desire. In so doing, other people's desires become models for us. Desire focuses on objects that other people already desire. In other words, desire is infectious. People look to others for clues to the proper object of their own desire. How else could we account for consumer phenomena such as the old "pet rock" craze? A pet rock has value only because other people desire it. How else could we account for people being murdered for a pair of Nike sneakers?

Borrowing Desire: "Keeping up with the Joneses" entails keeping up with their desires, not merely their property. We do not primarily desire the property of another. What we actually seek is to make the very desire of another our own personal property. By borrowing someone else's desire, we obtain a self-sufficiency that we lack. The phrase "get a life" aptly describes the mimetic process. One sure way to get a life is to borrow someone else's. The structure of mimetic desire involves a triangle of: (1) the object of desire, (2) the self or subject who desires the object, and (3) the model who elicits the subject's desire for the object of desire in the first place. The Joneses are the abstract model we all keep up with. The structure of desire looks like this:

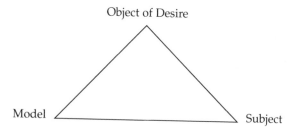

Object of Desire

Model

Subject

The Structure of Desire: Within this structure, no one desires anything directly, but only through the mediation of someone else's desire. The phenomenon of borrowed desire provides a clue to what makes markets. Whenever we borrow desire, we remain in debt to the model of our desire. The desiring subject is the debtor and the model is the creditor. The subject "owes" his or her desire to the model. The model attracts the "interest" of the subject in the first place. And, like all creditors, the model cannot resist the urge to charge "interest" on this desire. Borrowed desire is self-perpetuating. Like deficit spending, it produces instant results, but more somber long-range consequences.

Adam and Eve and Advertising: As far back as the Garden of Eden, Eve did not recognize the desirability of the fruit of the tree of the knowledge of good and evil until the serpent pointed it out to her. The serpent mediated her desire. Keeping up with the Joneses presupposes an attentive ear to the serpent. Obviously the entire focus of the advertising industry lies in eliciting and exploiting borrowed desire. Television advertising proves that you do not sell your product by emphasizing the product, but by emphasizing the "models" in the ad who are selling the product (e.g., basketball stars, movie stars, Marlboro men, etc.). Jerry Thomas, president of a national research marketing company, explains why advertising works.

> Advertising can create a model people wish to identify with and imitate. The modeling instinct is one of the most powerful impulses in the psyche. Children model after their parents. Employees model after their bosses. We all imitate people we admire. We are all copycats, though most of us are not aware of

just how much. Advertising can create personalities and im-
ages that trigger the modeling instinct. The "Marlboro Man" is
a classic example of a psychological archetype people have
chosen to identify with in cigarette brand choice.[8]

The reason advertising works is because the structure of
human desire is mimetic. One famous example of the power of
advertising is the tobacco market in Europe. This market was
dominated for decades by Turkish tobacco. Some analysts
have argued that the image of the Marlboro Man can justly
claim to have conquered the market single-handedly. Many
men in Europe took the Marlboro Man as their model.

The Scarlett O'Hara Syndrome: Another example of triangular desire is from the world of romance. In the modern romance, *Gone With the Wind*, Scarlett O'Hara is the living
embodiment of borrowed desire. The beginning of the story
portrays her obsession with having the one man in her clois-
tered world that she cannot have—Ashley Wilkes. Scarlett's
interest in Ashley reaches its apex after she discovers he is en-
gaged to another woman, Melanie Hamilton. Melanie is the
model that exacerbates Scarlett's desire for Ashley. Remember
the classic scene where Rhett Butler "snoozes" on a couch unseen by Scarlett and Ashley. Scarlett professes her adoration of
Ashley in an attempt to get him to call off his engagement to
Melanie. The triangle of Scarlett, Ashley, and Melanie awakens
Rhett's own desire for Scarlett. Ashley is the model that moves
Rhett's desire for Scarlett. Triangular desire is contagious and
tends to generate other triangles. This is literally how "markets" are formed, how objects that were previously not desired
become desired. The *ménage à trois* is the perfect image of the
market.

Seduction and Self-Destruction: Self-destruction is built
into the game of desire. Seduction is not a matter of love—it is
a poker game that is primarily competitive and secondarily
physical. (This art is best portrayed in the novel and movie,
Dangerous Liaisons. However, *Gone With the Wind* provides a
more accessible example of borrowed desire.) Girard describes
the game of seduction as similar to the game of dice.

> Desire has its own logic, and it is a logic of gambling. Once past a certain level of bad luck, the luckless player does not give up; as the odds get worse, he plays for higher stakes. Likewise, the subject [the lover] will always manage to track down the obstacle that cannot be surmounted . . . and he will destroy himself against it.[9]

Seduction is basically the game of playing hard to get, making the other partner show his or her cards (that is, his or her desire) first. Whoever appears god-like, self-sufficient, and "poker-faced," making the other partner grovel, is the winner. This showing of one's cards might be termed "the humiliating spectacle of one's own desire."[10] In the game of love, Scarlett practiced an asceticism of desire with Rhett—the hiding of her own desire in order to maintain the upper hand. In the case of Scarlett and Rhett, Scarlett never showed her cards, but Rhett finally tired of playing poker.

The Dilemma of Desire: The danger in the game of seduction is that the lover who first says "I love you" risks having his or her desire imitated by the beloved. If the beloved who hears the impassioned plea, "I love you," mimics the desire of the lover and translates that statement into "I love myself," then the beloved will conclude that the lover is unworthy of the beloved's affections.[11] The first confession of the lover bids up the value of the beloved to the point where the beloved becomes unattainable. This same dilemma in the art of seduction occurs in the business world's art of negotiation.

Borrowed Desire at the Office and in the Market

Desire at Salomon Brothers: Negotiating forms the heart of office politics. The funniest description of office politics comes from the writings of bond trader turned financial columnist, Michael Lewis. Lewis's *Liar's Poker* has been called the true life equivalent of Tom Wolfe's *Bonfire of the Vanities*. Lewis's memoirs recount a hilarious (and often pathetic) trip through the 1980s world of Wall Street investment banking, where he learned the general law of borrowed desire at Salomon Brothers.

> If Salomon Brothers creates a new kind of bond or stock, within twenty-four hours Morgan Stanley, Goldman Sachs and the rest will have figured out how it worked and will be trying to make one just like it. I understand this as part of the game. I recall that one of the first investment bankers I met taught me a poem: God gave you eyes, plagiarize. A handy ditty when competing with other firms. What I was about to learn, however, is that the poem was equally handy when competing within Salomon Brothers.[12]

Desire in the Job Market: Lewis's first problem with landing a job in the bond department at Salomon Brothers was getting a managing director to take him on as a young trainee. Salomon Brothers hired employees generically and put them through a training program. It was up to the trainee to find a specific job within the jungle of Salomon Brothers. Lewis's apprenticeship in this process is a casebook study of borrowed desire.

> A managing director grew interested [in a trainee] only if he believed you were widely desired. Then there was a lot in you for him. A managing director won points when he spirited away a popular trainee from other managing directors. The approach of many a trainee, therefore, was to create the illusion of desirability. Then bosses wanted him, not for any sound reason, but simply because other bosses wanted him. The end result was a sort of Ponzi scheme of personal popularity, that had its parallels in the markets. A few weeks into the training program I made a friend on the trading floor, though not in the area in which I wanted to work. That friend pressed me to join his department. I let other trainees know that I was pursued. They told their friends on the trading floor, who in turn became curious. Eventually, the man I wanted to work for overheard others talking about me and asked me to breakfast.[13]

Lewis's experience is reminiscent of professional basketball and football teams that delight in stealing star players from each other. Needless to say, Lewis got the job he wanted. He learned the art of becoming desirable and created a market for himself. The same technique is used by Tom Sawyer to get his neighbors to paint Aunt Polly's fence for him. Tom pretends that whitewashing fences is the greatest job in the world and soon has the entire neighborhood fighting over who gets to paint the fence.

Desire in the Stock Market: The stock market exhibits this same peculiar behavior and carries it to global dimensions. The quest for the secret mechanism of the market has generated a mountain of research but not much consensus. Some analysts argue passionately that fundamental economic values are the ultimate foundation of stock prices in the market (fundamental analysts). Others counter that there is no fundamental basis for stock values; there are only statistical patterns of past price changes that can be used to predict future price fluctuations (technical analysts). Another group of analysts (random walk theorists) argue that the market is too efficient to consistently outguess. And, of course, these analysts have their opponents who argue that the market is grossly inefficient and opportunities abound (e.g., George Soros).[14]

Picking Pretty Faces: The theory of borrowed desire offers a different approach to stock market analysis by positing a mimetic theory of value. This theory is hinted at by the liberal economist, John Maynard Keynes. In describing the bizarre behavior of the investment world, Keynes likens it to a particular kind of beauty contest (that newspapers used to run in the early 1900s) in which the contestants pick the face that they think other contestants will pick. Picking stocks is like picking pretty faces.

> Professional investment may be likened to those newspaper competitions in which the competitors have to pick out the six prettiest faces from a hundred photographs, the prize being awarded to the competitor whose choice most nearly corresponds to the average preference of the competitors as a whole; so that each competitor has to pick, not those faces which he himself finds prettiest, but those which he thinks likeliest to catch the fancy of the other competitors, all of whom are looking at the problem from the same point of view. It is not a case of choosing those which, to the best of one's judgment, are really the prettiest, not even those which average opinion genuinely thinks the prettiest. We have reached the third degree

where we devote our intelligences to anticipating what average opinion expects average opinion to be. And there are some, I believe, who practice the fourth, fifth and higher degrees.[15]

The theory of mimetic desire exhibits an explanatory power, if not a predictive power, that eludes the traditional market explanations of fundamental analysis, technical analysis, and random walk theory.

THE DOUBLE-BIND AND THE MANAGEMENT COMPLEX

Borrowed Desire's Internal Conflict: Since desire is mediated by the desire of another, conflict is built into the structure of desire. The model's desire, which initially elicits a desire in the subject, remains ambivalent. Although flattered by the imitation, the model is protective of his or her own desire. What if the subject's desire is stronger than the model's, and the subject ends up with the coveted object of the model's desire? While the "eternal husband" is flattered by other men's attentions to his wife, what happens when his wife is equally flattered?

Co-Dependency Between Subject and Model: Triangular desire breeds rivalry between model and subject or model and disciple. The model and disciple are co-dependent on each other's desire.

> Rivalry does not arise because of the fortuitous convergence of two desires on a single object; rather, *the subject desires the object because the rival desires it.* In desiring an object the rival alerts the subject to the desirability of the object.[16]

Mimetic desire creates a conflict that the psychiatrist Gregory Bateson refers to as the "double bind."[17] The double bind is a "contradictory double imperative" that the model imposes on the imitator. Embedded in the bind are two commands: (a) "Imitate me! Desire what I desire!" and (b) "Don't imitate me! Don't appropriate my object!" In the adulterous triangle of the *Eternal Husband,* the husband both encourages and repels the attentions of his wife's lovers. He is trapped because he cannot find his wife desirable unless other men find her desirable.

The Oedipus Complex and the Double-Bind: Freud's famous Oedipus Complex illustrates borrowed desire and the double-bind. The Oedipal triangle consists of mother, son, and father. Anthropologists have questioned the universality of Freud's Oedipus Complex for decades. But, whereas Freud emphasizes the object of the Oedipus Complex (the mother as sexual object), Girard emphasizes the mimetic rivalry itself. The son's identification with his father puts him in a "double bind." He must imitate his father in order to mature, and he must not imitate his father in order to mature. The son's super-ego tells him:

> "You ought to be like this (like your father)."

The son's super-ego also tells him:

> "You may not be like this (like your father)—that is, you may not do all that he does; some things are his prerogative."[18]

Like gravity, mimesis is both a force of attraction and a force of repulsion—thus the double-bind. Imitation begins in innocent apprenticeship, progresses to obsessive rivalry, and graduates to violence.

The Management Complex (Simple Diagram): The double-bind also forms the heart of employer-employee relations. Consider the triangle of the Management Complex:

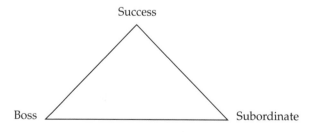

The boss is both the ticket to the top and the major obstacle to the employee's promotion or success. Similarly a productive employee helps the boss climb the ladder, whereas an unproductive employee reflects badly on the boss. The relationship between boss and employee contains as much ambivalence as the relationship of parent and offspring in the Oedipus Complex or the Electra Complex. But few people go to therapy to work out their Management Complex.

Managerial Schizophrenia: As in the relationship of parent and child in the Oedipus Complex, the employee must imitate the boss in order to succeed, and the employee must not imitate the boss in order to succeed. Like the parent to the child, the boss is constantly sending out double messages to the employee: "Be assertive. Don't be assertive." "Take initiative. Don't make a mistake." "Make me look good. Don't upstage me." "Take risks. Follow the rules." To give the boss due credit, the boss is also receiving these double messages from his or her own boss. And the employee is passing these double messages down the line to other subordinates. Furthermore, the boss is in a double-bind with respect to the delicate balance of delegation and control. If the boss delegates too much responsibility, the boss loses control. If the boss micro-manages employees, the bosses hinders productivity. With all these double messages being generated, it is little wonder that office politics becomes a jungle.

The Peter Principle: The double-bind of the Management Complex bears close resemblance to the popular conundrum known as the Peter Principle. "In a hierarchy, every employee tends to rise to his (her) level of incompetence."[19] Employees approach their level of incompetence by struggling to become "like their boss." This unproductive behavior of imitating the boss contradicts the simple economic law of the "division of labor." Specialization of labor yields higher total output because labor can become more skilled at particular tasks. Bill Gates argues that IBM's inattention to this principle cost them market share in the emerging field of PC software.

> IBM was such a great company. Why did it have so much trouble with PC software development? One answer is that IBM tended to promote all of its good programmers into management and leave the less talented behind.[20]

The Division of Labor: To the extent that everyone in a hierarchy struggles to be the same (to be "like the boss"), the specialization that boosts productivity will suffer. When employees finally become "like their bosses," they must sacrifice those unique qualities that got them hired in the first place (hence their rise to the level of incompetence). Productive bosses surround themselves with employees that possess the skills they lack. They encourage diversity and resist the universal temptation to hire people that are like them. Productive employees will be very different from their bosses and not necessarily equipped to step into their shoes. The Management Complex tends to destroy this productive division of labor.

The Eclipse of the Desired Object: The complexity of the double-bind does not stop with the frustrations caused by the double message. The conflict itself gradually becomes something to which both model and subject are attracted. The attraction that this conflict generates is the key to understanding how competition is a form of idolatry. The object of desire quickly takes a back seat to the rivalry itself.[21] Competitors become obsessed with each other rather than with the "things" they are competing for. In fact their very rivalry establishes the value of the things they want. The degree of struggle encountered in acquiring things is directly proportionate to their value. The heart of capitalism is not materialism, but borrowed desire—competition for competition's sake. Borrowed desire is pure competition.

The Dilemma of Competition: The dilemma of competition centers on the fact that rivalry produces value. For the sake of argument, assume that a boss and her subordinate are both competing to work on the same project. The subordinate's desire for the opportunity is heightened due to the perceived superiority of the boss/model. If the boss withdraws from the competition and the subordinate wins the assignment, then the assignment loses its prestige. On the other hand, if the subordinate loses the assignment to the boss, then the value of the project increases in the eyes of the subordinate. The left horn of the competitive dilemma is a loss of desire after winning—

a kind of buyer's remorse. The right horn of the dilemma is an increase in desire due to losing.[22] As Groucho Marx put the dilemma: "I never want to be a member of a club that would have me for a member!"

Competition as Idolatry: Because of the nature of borrowed desire, the idolization of the object is replaced by the idolization of the model. Consider the following analogy which describes the idolatrous nature of competition:

> A man sets out to discover a treasure he believes is hidden under a stone; he turns over stone after stone but finds nothing. He grows tired of such a futile undertaking but the treasure is too precious for him to give up. So he begins to look for a stone which is too heavy to lift—he places all his hope in that stone and he will waste all his remaining strength on it. . . . The impassioned person is seeking the divine through this insuperable obstacle, through that which, by definition, cannot be crossed.[23]

The stone is the rival, the competitor. Idolatry is a case of mistaken identity. We think we see God where God is not. An idol is anything or anyone that is not God, but is treated as if they were God. Denial of God does not do away with the transcendent, but merely transfers our passion for God from the divine realm to the human realm. "The imitation of Christ becomes the imitation of one's neighbor."[24] Idolatry entails this horizontal as opposed to vertical transcendence. The world of competition is a world of false gods. When the competitive phenomenon intoxicates us we "become gods in the eyes of each other." Like the ancient myth of Sisyphus, we are condemned for eternity to push stones (i.e., competitors) up a hill, only to have them roll back down, transformed into larger stones. The obsessive thinking of the competitor says: "If only I beat this rival, then I'll be saved." Then another rival comes along and the game must be played over again. This phenomenon might be classified as a religious addiction.

Objection to the Mimetic Theory: The mimetic theory has often been criticized for reducing complex phenomena to one simple idea. In other words, although the theory may be true, it is exaggerated. For example, when people desire hamburgers, it is not always because they just saw someone else eating a hamburger—this is absurd. Sometimes people want hamburgers simply because they are hungry. (Sometimes a cigar is just a cigar.) However, simple desires are easily inflamed into more complex desires. Desire is contagious. One evening I may eat three hamburgers, instead of one because of the influence of advertising. Or I may eat three hamburgers instead of one because I was passed over for promotion at work. It is not always easy to distinguish the emptiness in my stomach from the emptiness in my self. Once we confuse what we need with what we want, we have an ethical problem. The exaggeration of simple desire through the mimetic process creates these problems. And these are the problems that are of particular interest to the field of business ethics.

Notes

1. John and Sylvia Ronsvalle, *The Poor Have Faces: Loving Your Neighbor in the 21st Century* (Grand Rapids, Mich.: Baker Book House, 1991) 53–4.

2. Karl Marx, *Economic and Philosophic Manuscripts of 1844* (Moscow: Progress Publishers, 1974) 104.

3. Max Weber, *The Protestant Ethic and the Spirit of Capitalism* (New York: Charles Scribner's Sons, 1958) 60.

4. Jean-Michel Oughourlian, *The Puppet of Desire* (Stanford, Calif.: Stanford University Press, 1991) 3.

5. René Girard, *Things Hidden Since the Foundation of the World* (Stanford, Calif.: Stanford University Press, 1987) 9. Hereafter cited as THFW.

6. Aristotle, *Nicomachean Ethics*, I, 3.

7. George Bernard Shaw, *Man and Superman*, Act IV.

8. Jerry Thomas, "Why Advertising Works," *Business First* (September 9, 1996) 29.

9. René Girard, THFW, 298.

10. René Girard, *Deceit, Desire, and the Novel* (Baltimore: Johns Hopkins University Press) 160. Hereafter cited as DDN.

11. Paisley Livingston, *Models of Desire: René Girard and the Psychology of Mimesis* (Baltimore: Johns Hopkins University Press, 1992) 53.

12. Michael Lewis, *Liar's Poker: Rising Through the Wreckage on Wall Street* (New York: W. W. Norton & Co., 1989) 186.

13. Ibid., 43.

14. See George Soros, *The Alchemy of Finance* (New York: Wiley & Sons, 1987) and "The Capitalist Threat," *Atlantic Monthly* 279, no. 2 (February 1997). Soros goes so far as to posit the claim that market prices are always wrong. There are similarities between Soros' analysis of market behavior in his theory of reflexivity and Girard's analysis of mob behavior in his theory of mimetic desire.

15. John Maynard Keynes, *The General Theory of Employment, Interest and Money* (London: Macmillan, 1936) 156. Quoted in André Orléan's "Money and Mimetic Speculation," in Paul Dumouchel, ed. *Violence and Truth: On the Work of René Girard* (Stanford, Calif.: Stanford University Press, 1988) 105.

16. René Girard, *Violence and the Sacred* (Baltimore: Johns Hopkins University Press, 1977) 145. Hereafter cited as VS.

17. See Gregory Bateson, "Towards a Theory of Schizophrenia" in *Steps to An Ecology of Mind* (New York: Ballantine Books, 1972).

18. Sigmund Freud, "The Ego and the Id," in the *Standard Edition of the Complete Psychological Works*, vol. 19 (London: Hogarth Press, 1961) 34.

19. Laurence J. Peter and Raymond Hull, *The Peter Principle: Why Things Always Go Wrong* (New York: William Morrow, 1969) 26.

20. Bill Gates, *The Road Ahead* (New York: Penguin Books, 1995) 64.

21. To be precise, the innocent phenomenon of mimesis develops into the drama of mimetic desire when the object of desire is replaced by a fixation with the model. Mimesis itself is good because it opens us out of ourselves into relationship with other people.

22. See Paisley Livingston, op. cit., 89.

23. René Girard, DDN, 176 and 182.

24. Ibid., 59.

CHAPTER 5

The Secret of Management: Blame

Behind every great fortune lies a crime.

Honore de Balzac

No good deed goes unpunished.

Clare Boothe Luce

In the corporate world, 1,000 "Attaboys" are wiped away with one "Oh, shit!"

Robert Jackall

CONFLICT RESOLUTION BY SACRIFICE

Compensation Envy: The greatest danger in the Management Complex is that employees lose sight of their product and their customers. The obsession "to be the boss" can become all consuming. The frustrated employee suffers from (to paraphrase Freud) a terminal case of "compensation envy." The employee can always look at the boss's compensation package and say, "His is bigger than mine!"

Summary of the Management Complex: But, if the problem is the desire "to be the boss," why not just renounce the desire "to be the boss"? This is a tempting answer, but the Management Complex is more difficult to untangle than that. Like the employee, the boss is also insecure in his or her desire. One of the ways the boss finds reassurance is in the envy of the employees. "I must be on the right track . . . everyone wants to be like me." Even though the employee's desire to be the boss threatens the boss, the lack of this desire is equally threatening. It is an insult to the boss's status if an employee does not aspire to that same status—or at least appear to. The authors of *The Peter Principle* emphasize the "paramount importance of concealing the fact that you want to avoid promotion."[1] Indifference to the boss's status is just as dangerous as the craving for the boss's status. The boss, like the apple in the Garden of Eden, is the forbidden fruit. Even in an organization of professionals where there are many bosses or partners (e.g., accountants, lawyers, investment advisors), this Catch-22 focuses on those "stars" in the system who are ritually idolized each year at bonus time.

Oedipus and Management Complex Compared: So how is the Management Complex resolved? It is helpful to compare it to the Oedipus/Electra Complex. The child begins to resolve the complex by eventually leaving home and successfully establishing a home of his/her own with the right spouse. How does the employee resolve the Management Complex? In many businesses, there is no way for the employee to "leave home" without finding a new job. Admittedly, in a growing company there is some opportunity for promotion or "leaving home" while staying within the company. But of course this remains an illusion for most employees who will never get beyond the glass ceiling. Someone has to be at the bottom. In fact, most people have to be there. However, the token promotion provides the hope that keeps the rest of us going, at least for awhile.

Resolution of Management Complex: Imagine an extended group of overlapping triangles—dozens of employees imitating each others' desires. Double-binds multiply at exponential rates. In order to find a solution to the Management Complex, employees must transform their frustrated desire for promotion (which they cannot all have) into something else. As employees realize that others share their own frustrations, the

group develops a sense that some injustice has been committed. But, wherever there is a crime, there must be a criminal.
So, the group begins to focus its generalized sense of injustice
into a unified desire for someone to blame. By diverting its
competitive rivalries onto a scapegoat, the group replaces the
object of its frustrated desire (the promotion) that cannot be
shared with an object of hatred that can be shared. Group violence is one resolution of the Management Complex.

The Management Complex (Extended Diagram): The plot of
this triangular drama moves from: (1) a desire for the same object, (2) to a preoccupation with the rivalry itself, (3) to the
search for a scapegoat to resolve the crisis.

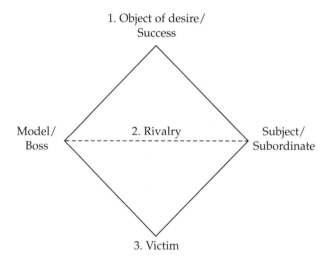

In the Management Complex, the frustrated "acquisitive"
desire of the top triangle evolves into the unanimous "ac-
cusatory" desire of the bottom triangle. The driving force in
both triangles is the same—desire borrowed from others. In
this light, the scapegoating mechanism is revealed as borrowed hatred. But to borrow hatred from others and destroy
the reputation or career of an innocent scapegoat can be explained in terms of primitive religious impulses.

Sacred Origins of Sacrifice: In order to understand these impulses, we must digress to examine the practice of sacrifice in general. While hardly a topic suitable for polite dinner conversation, the fact that human and animal sacrifice still holds a contemporary fascination can be attested to by the recent popularity of Joseph Campbell's *The Power of Myth*, a book that dwells extensively on the intricacies of sacrificial rites.

Sacrifice in New Guinea: Consider one of Campbell's particularly gruesome stories of ritual violence:

> There is a ritual associated with the men's societies in New Guinea. . . . The young boys who are being initiated into manhood are now to have their first sexual experience. There is a great shed of enormous logs supported by two uprights. A young woman comes in ornamented as a deity, and she is brought to lie down in this place beneath the great roof. The boys, six or so, with the drums going and the chanting going, one after another, have their first experience of intercourse with the girl. And when the last boy is with her in full embrace, the supports are withdrawn, the logs drop, and the couple is killed. . . . Then the little couple is pulled out and roasted and eaten that very evening.[2]

According to Campbell, this ritual follows a pattern of death and resurrection that is universal in primitive mythology. The young couple must die in order for the next planting season to be successful. The collective business of the primitive tribe cannot succeed in the coming season without the sacrifice of an innocent scapegoat. Maybe we have not all come so far?

Why Sacrifice?   There is little agreement among anthropologists regarding the motivation for sacrifice. However, anthropologists often fall back on one of three explanations: "gift, communion, or expiation."[3] Sacrifice as gift carries the connotation of economic exchange. Sacrifice as gift may be understood as (1) either an attempt to bribe the gods into giving us what we want, or (2) as an expression of thanksgiving to the gods for their gifts to us. Sacrifice as communion entails the attempt of human beings to enter into a relationship with the divine by the physical assimilation of some sacred animal or plant. The connotation is not only that of sharing a meal with the gods, but of actually partaking of the substance of the gods. Sacrifice as expiation refers to the attempt to avert the anger or wrath of the gods by offering something valuable to them. This kind of self-sacrifice is offered to gain the sympathy of the gods.

Sacrifice as a Business Deal: It is easy to compare primitive rites and modern church practices. Over the course of history the entire phenomenon of sacrifice has gone through a series of substitutions; bloody sacrifices are gradually replaced by more symbolic sacrifices and rituals. And these rituals are often replaced by simple ascetical practices like giving something up for Lent. But what about the relation of primitive sacrifice to business? At least one of the theories of sacrifice, sacrifice as gift, portrays sacrifice as originally a business transaction with the gods. "Sacrifice was therefore originally a simple business transaction of *du ut des* ("I give so that you will give in return"), an activity without moral significance."[4] Sacrifice was simply a method of trading or bartering with the gods. Humans sacrificed a goat and received a good harvest of wheat in return. In the modern economy, money has become a symbolic substitute for the goat. One modern equivalent of this sacrificial act might be tithing at church. The age old dilemma in any church offering is whether the motive is gratitude or bribery. Is buying your boss a Christmas present that different?

Sacrifice Creates Culture: Girard also sees the practice of sacrifice as a kind of business transaction, but of a more complex nature than the theories of gift, communion, and expiation entail. Sacrifice is not a transaction with the gods, but with society. Sacrifice is a complex mechanism that creates and maintains social order, a safety valve that prevents social chaos by appeasing the mob rather than by appeasing the gods. Sacrifice channels the pent up hostility of society as a whole by bribing its members into an act of violence with the promise of peaceful co-existence (communion, if you will). In fact, sacrifice is the foundation of all culture—religious, business, and otherwise. Recall the old story of the shipwrecked man who, upon reaching land and discovering a gallows, remarks, "Thank God, civilization!"

Sacrifice Appeases Violence:　However, the goal of sacrifice is not violence, but peace. Sacrifice appeases rather than promotes violence by replacing the "war of all against all" (social chaos) with the solution of "all against one" (social order). Sacrifice, then, functions as an inoculation against the plague of "reciprocal" violence, the endless cycle of revenge. As a minute amount of disease provides a vaccination for the patient, so a minuscule amount of violence saves a community from its most socially communicable disease. Sacrifice purges the system of internal disorders; a little bloodletting prevents massive bloodshed. "When unappeased, violence seeks and always finds a surrogate victim. The creature that excited its fury is abruptly replaced by another, chosen only because it is vulnerable and close at hand."[5]

Violence without Risk:　Sacrifice is an act of "official" violence without the risk of vengeance. Those who may be sacrificed play a unique role in the community. Fringe dwellers are chosen as victims since they elicit little sympathy. No one is likely to come to an outsider's defense. Victims are expendable. In ancient sacrificial cultures, victims were beings on the fringe of society—animals, prisoners, slaves, foreigners, even kings. They were different either by virtue of being outcasts (e.g., prisoners) or by virtue of being highly exalted (e.g., kings). But anyone different from the general mob was vulnerable. In primitive monarchies kings were often treated royally at first, only to be tortured and killed at the end of their reign. Freud describes the ancient king as a scapegoat with a suspended sentence. "Worshipped as a god one day, he is killed as a criminal the next."[6]

The Pharmakos Syndrome:　The ancient Greeks incorporated the traits of the fringe dweller in their institution of the *pharmakos*. The *pharmakos* was typically a criminal awaiting capital punishment. He was marched through town before his sacrifice to absorb all the impurities and hostilities within the community. Athens kept at public expense a few of these unfortunate souls for emergency sacrifice. Plague, famine, foreign invasion, even internal dissension were occasions to produce one of these "professional" victims. (Our medical term "pharmacy" comes from such early sacrificial practice.) The *pharmakos* was both poison (the one blamed for all communal problems) and antidote (the one sacrificed for restoration of communal peace); he embodied a double transference of blame and restoration. The mob transferred their aggression onto the scapegoat, and after witnessing the pacifying effect of sacrifice on the community, the mob transferred their devotion to the same scapegoat. The scapegoat became an idol. All myths of a dying and rising god follow this pattern.

The Caiaphas Syndrome: The high priest in the Passion story of Christ, Caiaphas, is the sacrificer (and politician) *par excellence.* Caiaphas, more clearly than any other person in the Bible, understands that individuals must die unjustly in order to preserve the integrity of the political regime. Caiaphas believes that Jesus' popularity will alarm the Romans and threaten a retaliation against Israel (a reasonable concern considering what later happened to Israel). He addresses the chief priests:

> You do not seem to have grasped the situation at all; you fail to see that it is to your advantage that one man should die for the people, rather than that the whole nation should perish. (John 11:49-50)[7]

Contrast Caiaphas's logic to the parable of the straying sheep in which the shepherd abandons ninety-nine sheep to go in search of the one stray (Matt 18:12-14; Luke 15:3-7).

The Sacrificial Foundation of Human Institutions: Why must one man die? Because it works! Far from being a mystical affair, sacrifice provides a pragmatic solution to political tensions. Modern businesses employ this ancient religious practice. Sacrifice has saved many a corporation or country from all-out-war. War is an inefficient form of violence compared with sacrifice.[8]

BUSINESS CULTURE AS RELIGIOUS CULTURE

Sacrificial Management: Business culture is essentially religious. We are all told that if we work hard enough, we will succeed. Yet, we cannot all succeed, no matter how hard we work. In effect, all but a select few are necessarily failures. No matter how hard we try, we cannot all be "like Mike." Periodically, any group of employees will glimpse this Catch-22 which undermines the legitimacy of the business hierarchy. This realization is inherently destabilizing. A crucial factor in maintaining managerial control is having sacrificial individuals available when this occurs. Like Adam Smith's classic formula in which competition regulates rational self- interest, sacrifice is the mechanism that regulates irrational desire and keeps it from spinning out of control.

Decision as Sacrifice: The fundamental business of business is to make decisions. Even the most simple decisions close off all other options, in a sense sacrificing further dialogue and analysis. The conference table in a business meeting often functions like an altar. Issues and agendas are put on the table, sometimes with great passion. They cannot all be pursued. For the business to be run, some choices must be cut. The Latin origin of our word for decision, *decidere,* means "to hew off, to cut off." Decisions can have a decidedly sacrificial character. The very process of making a group decision around a table makes us vulnerable to our most primitive religious impulses.

Sacrificial Management: Peter Drucker alludes to sacrificial management in his description of the management style of Henry Luce, founder of *Time, Life,* and *Fortune.*[9] According to Drucker, Luce practiced a Chinese mandarin style of management—divide and conquer. Raised as a Chinese missionary's son, Luce did not live in America until he entered Yale. China, rather than America, molded Luce. His human relations, his way of managing, his system of control were Chinese. He emulated the ruler by remaining far from the scene of action and taking no direct part. Yet, no one else became a threat to his leadership because he cultivated factions and feuds among his subordinates. Franklin Delano Roosevelt used a strikingly similar management style. Roosevelt's maternal grandfather was a Chinese merchant, idolized by Roosevelt's powerful and domineering mother. From these traditional, family influences, Drucker concludes, Roosevelt formed his sacrificial management style. In such a system, the leader (or potential scapegoat) maintains power by making everyone else feel vulnerable.

CEO as High Priest: Another way of viewing business culture as a religious culture is to observe the priestly role of the modern executive. Once corporations achieve a certain level of size and complexity, it becomes almost impossible for the Chief Executive Officer to maintain a comprehensive understanding of the operations of the firm. The same is obviously true for government or any other bureaucracy. When this degree of complexity is crossed, the function of the CEO increasingly shifts from operations to public relations. Lee Iacocca has argued that the crucial task becomes one of image—convincing the troops, the shareholders, and the public that someone is in control of this massive complex. He attributes a great deal of his success at Chrysler to a skill as simple as speech making. The president of a complex corporation or of the U.S. occupies a "bully pulpit" where preaching becomes central.

Business as Theater: As Lewis Lapham argues, the successful CEO of a large corporation must exchange an empirical approach to business for a theatrical approach. The CEO must learn to acquire and combine "political instinct with a priestly function."[10] The function of the priest is to restore order to the community by appeasing the wrath of the gods (i.e., by sacrifice). Similarly, the function of the CEO is to bestow blame and credit on various people within the firm in order to reassure the troops that someone is in control. The problem is that it can take years and countless sacrificial lambs before the public or the shareholders discover that a CEO has lost touch with the fundamentals of the business. Some CEOs do and some do not. Lee Iacocca is a perfect example of someone who made the shift from operations to public theater without losing all the knowledge he gained as an engineer.

Violence as Two-Way Street: It should be emphasized that sacrifice and violence are not the preserve of "the boss" alone. To paraphrase Freud, the boss is often a scapegoat with a suspended sentence. Violence is a two-way street. Managers can be held hostage by workers that know how to play the game more astutely. The role of victim is often played in a shrewd bid for power. The power of the "authorities" always co-exists in an uneasy alliance with the power of the "mob."

> Those who are conservative try to consolidate the constituted authorities, the institutions that embody the continuation of a religious, cultural, political, and judicial tradition. They are susceptible to criticism for their excessive bias toward the established powers. They are equally susceptible to threats of violence from the crowd. For the revolutionaries the reverse is true. They systematically criticize institutions and shamelessly revere the violence of the crowd.[11]

The modern movement for "tort" reform in our society illustrates this tension between authorities and mob. It has become commonplace to describe our society as a society of victims. Everyone is vying for victim status. Remember the elderly lady who spilled McDonald's coffee in her lap and successfully sued McDonald's for a tidy sum. The jury awarded her less than $200,000 in compensatory damages, but added $2,700,000 in punitive (sacrificial?) damages. Here the corporate institution itself becomes the scapegoat—the authorities are sacrificed. And, of course, such legal expenses are ultimately passed on to the consumer, the final victim in this game.

MYTHS AS BLAMING SYSTEMS

Sacrifice Justified by Myth: Since the sacrificial system is so obviously unjust, how is it legitimized? According to Girard, mythology rationalizes sacrifice. Sacrifice works efficiently only if the crowd does not perceive that the victim is randomly selected. The crowd must firmly believe in the guilt of the victim and clearly perceive the victim's responsibility for whatever crime needs to be avenged. It is always the function of the crowd to shout "crucify him, crucify him."

Myth as the Science of Blame: Myth not only legitimizes sacrifice; it also explains the existence of failure. Failure is to the business world what sin is to the religious world. In business, failure is sin! But, since statistically, business failures far exceed business successes, how do we account for failure? This is the age-old religious question of Job: "why is there evil?"

Why Is There Evil? When people suffer and ask this question, they are not seeking scientific answers. When cancer patients ask, "why is this happening to me?" they are not interested in a medical treatise. People want a *personal* answer to this question. "Why is there evil?" readily translates into: "What did I do to deserve this?" "Why did I fail?" "Why do bad things happen to good people, i.e., me?" Michael Lewis wittily translates this question into: "Why do bad things happen to rich people?" When people inquire into the problem of evil, they want to know *what* is responsible for their pain?

Who Is Responsible for Evil? This inquiry easily slips over into another question: *who* is responsible for my pain? Who can I blame for my pain? Who deserves to pay for the pain I experience? Of course, this pain can be anything—unrequited love, business failures, humiliations suffered, or actual physical pain. The explanation we seek is really an expiation. "What caused my pain?" becomes "who will pay for my pain?" The mythology surrounding a sacrificial victim satisfies our moral outrage. Blaming the bubonic plague on the Jews' poisoning well water in the Middle Ages is a case in point. Blaming a business failure on the trade deficit, on the federal government, or on the mysterious actions of the Fed, are all modern examples.

Blame Explains: In mythological thought, blaming is a form of explaining. Myths, then, are "blaming systems." They help make sense of suffering by providing a reason for suffering. This need to explain suffering is crucial. As Nietzsche says, "What makes people rebel against suffering is not really suffering itself but the senselessness of suffering."[12] Blaming systems attempt to make suffering "intelligible." These systems can be sophisticated or primitive. Blaming the Jews for the bubonic plague is a primitive blaming system. Likewise, the Ku Klux Klan's blaming African-Americans for problems in Southern society illustrates a primitive blaming system.

Modern Myths: With the advent of the social sciences, such as sociology, psychology, and economics, more sophisticated blaming systems develop in order to explain suffering. Marxists blame capitalism for all the evils in the world. Capitalists blame government regulation for all the evils in the world. Feminists blame patriarchy. Conservatives blame secular humanism or multiculturalism. Liberals blame fundamentalism. Environmentalists blame "speciesism." Blacks blame racism. Whites blame affirmative action. Democrats and Republicans blame each other. Just about everybody blames the federal government! The list goes on and on. None of these blaming systems are as crass as we present them here. They are all defended by mountains of research and statistics. But often this research merely confirms the axe it is meant to grind. As the old adage goes: "Statistics are like a lamppost to a drunk—they support a position, but they don't always illuminate." Statistics can be part of the legitimization process of a given mythology. These mythical social scientific approaches help us cope with the unfairness of life by finding something, or better, someone to blame. Myths help us make sense of the world. They create order and structure out of our experience.

Blame Creates Order: Blaming the victim provides emotional as well as intellectual satisfaction to the search for the origins of suffering. Violent acts against a victim are the foundations of culture. The literature of antiquity abounds with references to the violent origins of civilization. The first city in the Old Testament is founded by the murderer Cain. After Cain killed Abel and was marked by God, "he became [the] builder of a town, and he gave the town the name of his son Enoch" (Gen 4:17). Rome was founded after a case of fratricide. Romulus killed his brother Remus. Today of course, the language of the "gods" and "myths" is replaced by the jargon of social science and management trends. For example, Total

Quality Management and reengineering are myths adopted to justify corporate cost cutting and massive layoffs. These myths allow a new streamlined economic order to be founded by pruning the "deadwood."

ADAM AND EVE: THE ORIGINAL BLAME GAME

A Garden of Desires: As a final example of the Management Complex, we examine the most famous of all stories, the story of Adam and Eve. The drama of the Fall begins in Genesis 2:18 when God reveals to Adam that it is not good for Adam to be alone. God judges that Adam needs a helper. Therefore God creates a host of animals in what proves to be a fruitless attempt to provide a suitable companion for Adam (Gen 2:20). So, God creates Eve out of Adam's flesh, and Adam is finally pleased (Gen 2:23). Having been passed over for promotion, the serpent, the most subtle of the animals made by God for Adam (Gen 3:1), is envious of Eve's special place in Adam's life. The serpent initiates the drama of the Management Complex by awakening Eve's desire for the fruit of the tree of the knowledge of good and evil (Gen 3:6, 13). The serpent, through its own envy of Eve's place in Adam's life, arouses Eve's envy of God by assuring Eve that the fruit will make her like God (Gen 3:5). Eve, and Adam like her, suffers from a God Complex. They both want to be like God. It should be noted that no one person can be blamed for the Fall from paradise. Traditional male-oriented interpretations of the Fall which assert that Eve caused Adam to sin distort the biblical idea of the Fall. Both Adam and Eve are infected by the same mimetic desire of the serpent. The chronological sequence of the desire is insignificant.

The Original Blame Game: When God discovers Adam and Eve's disobedience, the scapegoating mechanism begins. Adam and Eve rightly claim that their desire was caused by another. The woman blames the serpent. "The devil made me do it." The man blames the woman. And, implicitly, the man blames God by pointing out that the woman God gave him (Gen 3:12) was the cause of his undoing. Giving Adam a helper was, after all, God's idea (Gen 2:18). A further insinuation of God's responsibility for the Fall is implied in the description of God's jealousy and protection of divine turf. God banishes Adam and Eve from the garden lest they "become like one of us in knowing good from evil" and lest they become like one of us in eating of the tree of life and thereby achieving immortality (Gen 3:22).

CALVIN AND HOBBES © Watterson. Dist. by UNIVERSAL PRESS SYNDICATE. Reprinted with permission. All rights reserved.

The Projection of Blame onto God: In Chapter One of Genesis, God clearly desires that Adam and Eve be "in our own image" and "in the likeness of ourselves" (Gen 1:26). Yet, in Chapter Three, God is fearful lest Adam and Eve become "like one of us" (Gen 3:22). The combined account perfectly mirrors the double-bind imposed by the Freudian father: Be like me! Don't be like me! By giving us two different accounts of the creation story, Genesis points to the complexity of the divine/human relationship. However, the double account also implies that the double-bind in Genesis is a projection of human envy. We project our envy onto God.

The God Complex: Borrowed desire or envy is clearly at the heart of the Fall. As the serpent is the most subtle of animals, envy is the most subtle of sins. A fundamental ambiguity lies at the heart of envy for it entails both admiration and resentment. The atheist philosopher, Jean-Paul Sartre, describes this fundamental human passion succinctly:

> The best way to conceive of the fundamental project of human reality is to say that man is the being whose project it is to be God. . . . Man fundamentally is the desire to be God.[13]

The Management Complex reflects the secret aspiration to be the Big Boss. As Sartre's atheism confirms, you do not need to believe in God in order to believe in the God Complex.

Conclusion of Chapter Five: How do we resolve the Management Complex that we all share? The next chapter returns to the everyday work world where we will investigate the blame game with an analysis of the phenomenon of gossip. Once this phenomenon is clarified, the resolution of the Management Complex in non-violent ways can begin.

Notes

1. Laurence J. Peter and Raymond Hull, *The Peter Principle: Why Things Always Go Wrong* (New York: William Morrow, 1969) 153.

2. Joseph Campbell, *The Power of Myth* (New York: Doubleday, 1988) 106.

3. Mary Barbara Agnew, "A Transformation of Sacrifice," *Worship* 61, no. 6 (November 1987) 500.

4. Mircea Eliade, ed., *The Encyclopedia of Religion,* vol. 12 (New York: Macmillan, 1987) 550.

5. René Girard, VS, 2.

6. Sigmund Freud, "Totem and Taboo," in the *Standard Edition of the Complete Psychological Works,* vol. 13 (London: Hogarth Press, 1961) 44.

7. Caiaphas's role in the death of Christ is no more indicative of Jewish responsibility for his death than Pilate's role is of Roman responsibility. Nor can Herod be said to be the primary executioner of John the Baptist. In each of these instances the political leaders manifest their subservience to the crowd. For Girard, the mob is the final judge, jury, and executioner of victims.

8. Digression on Girard and religion: According to Girard, the Gospels reveal the violent foundation of all human institutions, religion being one of those institutions. This revelation turned into the religious institution of Christianity by acquiring cultural forms that were alien to it. The purpose of Christ's message and the prophets of the Hebrew Scriptures was to demythologize, not legitimize, the sacrificial structure of human cultures. The revelation of the Gospels is a continuation of the revelation of the prophetic tradition in the Hebrew Scriptures. "Salvation comes from the Jews" (John 4:22).

9. Peter Drucker, *Adventures of a Bystander* (New York: Harper Collins, 1991) 223ff.

10. Lewis Lapham, *Money and Class in America: Notes and Observations on Our Civil Religion* (New York: Weidenfeld & Nicolson, 1988) 178.

11. René Girard, *The Scapegoat* (Baltimore: Johns Hopkins University Press, 1986) 115–6.

12. Friedrich Nietzsche, *The Birth of Tragedy and The Genealogy of Morals* (Garden City, N.Y.: Doubleday, 1956) 200.

13. Jean-Paul Sartre, *Existentialism and Human Emotions* (New York: Philosophical Library, 1957) 63.

PART TWO

Practice/*Askesis*

CHAPTER 6

The Currency of Blame and Credit: Gossip

We have met the enemy and he is us.

Pogo

Madness is rare in individuals—but in groups, parties, nations, and ages it is the rule.

Nietzsche

Ignorance loves company.

Peter Lynch

PASSING THE BUCK

Passing the Buck: An analysis of the first chapters of Genesis may seem a far cry from life in the corporate fast lane. But a moment's reflection or look at the daily paper should assure us that human nature has not changed significantly since the good old days of Adam and Eve. Adam and Eve were quite adept at "passing the buck."

> God asked, "Have you been eating of the tree I forbade you to eat?" Adam replied, "It was the woman you put with me; she gave me the fruit, and I ate it." Then God asked the woman, "What is this you have done?" The woman replied, "The serpent tempted me and I ate." (Gen 3:11-13)

The business world has been passing bucks back and forth ever since Adam and Eve began the game. In fact, Harry

Truman defined the business of management with his famous remark: "the buck stops here." Where the buck stops is where management starts. Management is always about blame and credit.

Money Follows Blame and Credit: The phrase "passing the buck" is revealing. The double-meaning in the slang word, "buck,"—a dollar or blame—implies a relationship between money and guilt. As Michael Lewis noted in *Liar's Poker:*

> There are two kinds of friction within Salomon Brothers. The first is generated by people fighting to pin blame upon one another when money is lost. The second is generated by people fighting to claim credit when money is made.[1]

One relationship between money and guilt is that profit and loss quickly become blame and credit. But blame and credit can generate profits and losses as well. The mere appearance of success or failure often breeds success or failure.

Reading Social and Commercial Ledgers: Just as money flows through financial markets, "blame and credit" flow through social or political markets. Political markets trade in the currency of blame and credit, the buying and selling of responsibility. But let the buyer beware; blame and credit tend to come in package deals and must be evaluated carefully. Today's idols tend to become tomorrow's scapegoats and vice-versa. The impulse to resist blame and to chase credit must be tempered to the realities of the political marketplace. The shrewd trader of political capital will recognize that other players' exaggerated fears of blame may create a buying opportunity. Taking blame in a situation where everyone else is overreacting against it will often lead to group relief and gratitude. This gratitude is literally a form of political "credit" or "capital" that is available for later use. Generously giving credit away in a situation where others overvalue it can also generate valuable "brownie points." On the other hand, whoever takes credit when everyone else is craving it or dumps blame when others fear it will be resented by the group. And you can rest assured that the group will hold onto that debt for later collection. *Caveat emptor!*

Buy Cheap and Sell Dear: In financial markets, the ultimate rule of thumb is "buy cheap and sell dear." In mimetic markets, the social transactions are trickier but the rule still applies: the *modus operandi* is buy credit and sell blame. The trick is to buy credit when it is undervalued and to sell blame when it is overvalued. But magnifying your credit and shedding your blame is only a general rule. As you climb the ladder of corporate success, tactics often require you to minimize your credit and accept blame that belongs to someone else (e.g., in certain transactions with your superiors). Buying blame (when it is cheap) can be a sign of willingness to handle responsibility that can later be traded in for credit (promotions, etc.), and selling credit (when it is dear) can be a sign of generosity with similar positive results. Whether you like it or not, each workday involves a number of active trades in the marketplace of blame and credit. Your score over time determines whether you are getting ahead or falling behind.

Blame Management: The "bottom line" impact of an unhealthy political culture is that it becomes unproductive. The blame game raises the cost of doing business by consuming employee hours, but even worse by raising the personal cost of risk-taking. There are two basic types of managers in the business world: blame managers and result managers. (The same obviously applies to workers.) Blame managers spend their time managing their own blame and credit, the blame and credit of their department, and the blame and credit of their company. Result managers spend their time managing the tasks necessary to produce a product or service.

DILBERT reprinted by permission of United Features Syndicate, Inc.

Risk Avoidance: If you work for a blame manager, you will think twice before taking initiative. The worst thing an employee of a blame manager can do is make a mistake. The blame game lowers risk-taking in a given business milieu. As Peter Lynch says about the investment world:

> Whoever imagines that the average Wall Street professional [institutional investor] is looking for reasons to buy exciting stocks hasn't spent much time on Wall Street. The fund manager is most likely looking for reasons not to buy exciting stocks. . . . Success is one thing, but *it's more important not to look bad if you fail.* There's an unwritten rule on Wall Street: "You'll never lose your job losing your client's money on IBM."[2]

If the investor loses money on a small, obscure stock, the investor is blamed for losing the money. If the investor loses money on a large, established stock, the stock is blamed but not the investor. "What's wrong with IBM lately?" So the blame game discourages productivity and encourages conformism and the status quo. The blame game is like the children's game of hot potato.

Risk Acceptance: Result managers, by contrast, know that you have to accept losses in order to make money. They accept risk-taking and do not punish their employees who make mistakes as long as the number of results exceeds the number of mistakes. To quote Peter Lynch again:

> If seven out of ten of my stocks perform as expected, then I'm delighted. If six out of ten of my stocks perform as expected, then I'm thankful. Six out of ten is all it takes to produce an enviable record on Wall Street.[3]

Gossip and Myth-Information

Office Politics: Playing the game of blame and credit takes an enormous amount of energy in most businesses. This game is played out through the medium of office gossip. Gossip functions both as myth and as a form of violence. All offices have prevailing mythologies that keep tabs on who is in and who is out, who is hot and who is not. These myths have very little to do with job performance, but unfortunately often have much to do with job security. How you are gossiped about is directly tied to your level of political capital.

Gossip as Myth: The function of myth is to channel and conceal the violence of the sacrificial mechanism. Myths purposely (if unconsciously) identify the victim *and* confuse the facts in order to justify group violence. While most people see mythology as a thing of the past, its modern usage can most clearly be glimpsed in the phenomenon of gossip. Gossip is the art of managing blame and credit. A common way to avoid being scapegoated is to pump up the chatter that scapegoats others. Of course, this often backfires.

Gossip as Violence: Gossip has strong similarities both with myth and mob violence. It resembles myth in that it is verbal, not physical violence. It resembles mob violence in that it is a group action against an individual. According to the sociologist, Donna Eder, gossip is "evaluative talk about a person who is not present."[4] Since the person being gossiped about is not present, he or she is an easy vehicle for group fantasy (whether positive or negative). The victim of gossip is a potential sacrificial victim or a potential group idol. Absent people are safe targets—there is no threat of retaliation.

Gossip as Black Market: The "grapevine" of office gossip is a black market in information that continually reacts to official information. "Office culture" is manufactured within this black market. Gossip trades in whatever cannot be traded in the official office culture. Because the official rules of office culture tend to be unwritten and rigid, each person's perception of the rules will define where the black market begins. Ironically, the very secrecy of the gossip mill makes it a more powerful means of communication. Many management seminars on how to supervise employees encourage you to "compliment your employees behind their backs"—a more powerful compliment than complimenting them to their faces. Complimenting people behind their backs magnifies the compliment because the person being complimented senses the approval of a larger unseen audience. More people are involved in second-hand communication than in first-hand communication. One manager we worked with said that her rule of thumb was to criticize employees to their faces and compliment them behind their backs. This technique subdued the criticism and magnified the compliment. It should be noted that supervisory review provides an official monopoly on gossip. The better the official evaluation system is, the less gossip there will be. Supervisory review is a perfect time to compliment employees to their face.

The Gossip Triangle: Similarly, criticizing people behind their backs magnifies the criticism, because the person being criticized senses the denunciation of an unseen and unapproving audience. Second-hand criticisms are more threatening than first-hand criticisms because the victim of gossip never knows how many people shared the second-hand criticism. The first phase of gossip, the original denunciation behind someone's back, resembles mob violence. The second phase of gossip, the repetition of the original denunciation, follows the repetitious pattern of religious rituals. Gossip betrays a triangular structure of: (1) the victim being gossiped about, (2) the accuser originating the criticism, and (3) the messenger transmitting the criticism second-hand.

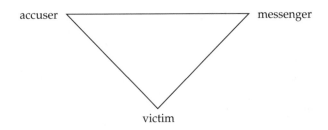

The messenger mimics the accuser by relaying the negative message. Of course if the gossip backfires against the accuser, the messenger is in a precarious situation for "they shoot the messenger of bad tidings."

The Positive Triangle: Of course, there can also be a more positive angle to the triangular structure of gossip:

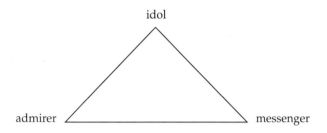

Here the triangle comprises: (1) the idol being gossiped about, (2) the admirer who originated the compliment, and (3) the messenger transmitting the compliment second-hand.

The Power of Gossip: The triangular structure of repeated gossip gives it its power. Direct communication is inherently more subdued because the mob is not present in direct communication. If you tell another man's wife that you are in love with her, there is no scandal because she is free to deal with the situation directly. If you tell your friends that you are in love with another man's wife, then the object of your affections must not only deal with you but with the rumor mill you started. The pledge of your affection suddenly has an entire audience behind it. You have put the object of your affection "on stage."

Gossip in the World of Romance: Shakespeare's comedies are charming lessons in the power of gossip.[5] The recent film version of Shakespeare's *Much Ado About Nothing* (starring Kenneth Branagh and Emma Thompson) shows the power of second-hand communication. Benedick and Beatrice are in love but afraid to confess their desire to each other. As in poker, each is reluctant to be the first to reveal their hand. They both sense danger in being the first one to say "I love you." The lover who plays "hard to get" possesses a mysterious power that the more vocal lover lacks. Since both Beatrice and Benedick are equally astute, they hide their desire behind a constant battle of wits.

Don Pedro's Technique: The shrewd prince, Don Pedro, realizes that the only way these two reluctant lovers can be persuaded of the other's affection is by having each of them overhear the other's proclamation of love. The rumor of love will be more effective than an open proclamation of love. So Don Pedro arranges for Benedick to overhear that Beatrice is madly in love with him and for Beatrice to overhear that Benedick is madly in love with her. The conspiracy succeeds and Benedick and Beatrice finally work up the courage (humility?) to openly confess their love to each other. Their love conquers their pride, but only by the ruse of second-hand communication. Of course the second-hand communication bestows the blessings of the crowd on the match.

Gossip in the World of Finance: Peter Lynch describes this phenomenon of gossip in the financial world. People lose money in the stock market because they are more attracted by the glitter of rumor than by the sobriety of information. Rumors have a glamour that might be termed "myth-information."

> Rumors, I know, are still more exciting than public information, which is why a snippet of conversation overheard in a restaurant—"Goodyear is on the move"—carries more weight than Goodyear's own literature. It's the old oracle at work: the more mysterious the source, the more persuasive the advice. Investors continually put their ears to the walls when it's the handwriting that tells everything. Perhaps if they stamped the annual and quarterly reports "classified" or mailed them out in plain brown wrappers, more recipients would browse through them.[6]

We propose the following hypothesis of mob behavior that parallels Peter Lynch's oracle: "The more removed from reality (i.e. from the initial source) a rumor is, the more powerful it becomes." A second-hand rumor is more seductive than direct communication; a third-hand rumor more powerful than a second-hand; a fourth-hand rumor more powerful than a third-hand, etc. Each movement of the rumor away from its source gives the rumor a credence of authority (i.e., the authority of the mob). This is because of the perception that the mob is growing and the circle is closing.

Gossip as Sacrifice: Gossip is an invitation to sacrifice or idol worship. Successful sacrifice presupposes no threat of reprisal from the victim's allies. If you are uncertain about how much clout (political capital) your potential victim might have, you leak your animosity in the form of gossip to test the reactions of the mob. Rumors are insurance that the shirt fits the back of the victim. The invitation is necessary to gather the congregants to worship. Gossip is a concrete example of how the Management Complex expresses itself.

Triangulation: In one privately owned company we visited, gossip in the central office became so destructive that management began a campaign to prohibit such talk. Office personnel wore buttons that looked like this:

The prohibition against gossip was visualized as NO TRIANGULATION! The structure of gossip gives a micro-analysis to the behavior of the mob.

Mob Behavior

The Mob as Truth: The most disturbing characteristic of mob behavior is the ability of the mob to dominate public opinion. As the political columnist Hedrick Smith says (quoting E. E. Schattschneider): "If a fight starts, watch the crowd because the crowd plays the decisive role."[7] Contests are more often decided by the crowd than by the contestants. The rumors of the mob become the final arbiter of truth. Psychologists refer to this peculiar aspect of mob behavior as the principle of social proof: "The greater the number of people who find any idea correct, the more the idea will be correct."[8] The more uncertainty reigns in a given social situation, the more people are likely to accept the actions and opinions of others as correct. The more complex our society becomes the more uncertainty prevails. To compensate for this complexity, people take mental shortcuts. One such shortcut is "social proof." None of us has the time to analyze the truth of all the opinions we are bombarded with. One solution is to accept as true what most people believe or what most people find enticing. This mental shortcut is exploited to the hilt by the entertainment and advertising industries. The proven effectiveness of canned laughter in sitcoms is one example.

The Dangers of Social Proof: Another example is the bystander phenomenon. Remember the story of the New York woman, Catherine Genovese, who was tortured and killed over a period of thirty minutes in earshot of thirty-eight of her neighbors. An anonymous call from any one of the neighbors to the police might have saved her life. It was not merely fear of reprisal that motivated the response of the neighbors. Nor was it merely apathy. It was uncertainty. Since none of the neighbors saw each other acting, they took the social cue that this situation was a non-emergency. "Since nobody is concerned, nothing is wrong."[9] This same phenomenon might account for the mass suicide instigated by the Reverend Jim Jones in Jonestown, Guyana or the mass suicide of the Heaven's Gate cult in southern California. Since everyone is committing suicide, it must be normal. These mass suicides portray extreme examples of what social scientists have dubbed "the Werther effect."[10] Studies show that, following highly publicized suicide stories, suicide rates increase dramatically in those geographic areas exposed to the publicity. Troubled people imitate the suicide as an acceptable form of behavior.

Business Cycles and Social Factions: Mob behavior follows certain patterns that might be seen as loosely analogous to business cycles. The business cycle is typically seen as an economic cycle of inflation, recession, productivity, and employment. Just as the business cycle mirrors the rise and fall of economic sectors, mob behavior mirrors the rise and fall of social factions. How do factions arise?

High School Factions: Think back to high school. A small group is standing around and one member says something negative about a fellow student who is not present. This comment operates like a "trial balloon." The group will either accept the invitation to gossip about the proposed victim or decline. Once the proposed victim is agreed upon, the victim becomes a defining characteristic of the group. The jocks know who they are by knowing who the nerds are. But this does not depend upon reality. More likely, the victim was chosen for personal reasons, e.g., the accuser's girlfriend was seen flirting with the proposed victim. But by the time the group is finished gossiping, the identity of the victim as nerd has been caricatured to suit the needs of the group. "We are people who are not like that." Social order is established by the sacrifice of the nerd. Nerds may form their own factions in retaliation. Other factions (whether musicians, rednecks, preppies, etc.) form in similar fashion.

Office Factions: It has been said that we never leave high school. Secretaries form factions based upon scapegoating an unpopular secretary or an unpopular boss. Middle management forms factions based upon departments or common personality types. The bean counters blame the spenders for all the company's ills and vice-versa. The decision makers blame the business analysts. The lawyers in compliance fight the sales force. And everyone blames personnel and vice-versa. Among senior management, the stakes are higher. All of these factions float their own trial balloons in the same way as individuals. Senior management is in charge of this "factional gossip." But the purpose is the same: to propose a common enemy for the purpose of creating a larger alliance. The process of sacrificing scapegoats is a dynamic, continually changing game. Individuals coalesce into cliques. Cliques become factions. Factions form alliances. The formation of all of these groups has a tendency to be based on a common enemy. It is a rare group that does not depend upon the occasional scapegoat for its continued cohesiveness. This is true in social groups, at the office, and in the marketplace as a whole.

Power Surfing: Just as it takes a shrewd investor to avoid the pitfalls of the business cycle, it takes a shrewd employee to avoid the sacrificial instincts of the mob. If you do not know who the next scapegoat is, it is probably you. For it is the instinct of the mob to chant, "crucify him, crucify him." What must be learned is a vigilant detachment from the fear of blame and the craving for credit. Fear and greed tend to blind the employee to the power game. This struggle is brilliantly described by the *Washington Post* columnist, Hedrick Smith, in his book, *The Power Game: How Washington Works.* Smith describes politicians as "surfers riding the waves of power." The waves of power are the waves of blame and credit that are constantly generated by the mob. Smith describes politicians:

> Sometimes they are careening at top speed before some giant wave; sometimes they are coasting slowly, looking for a crest. Their success depends on avoiding the thunderous surf around them. From time to time, they may have to make those agile sideward shifts that enable the most skilled surfers to escape being crashed beneath the waves.[11]

The way the politician keeps from being swallowed up in the waves of blame and credit is detachment.

The Example of Ronald Reagan: Of all people to teach about detachment, the most interesting is the late Lee Atwater, the modern campaign manager who understood the Caiaphas Syndrome perfectly. Atwater attributes President Reagan's success to his detachment from power. Reagan was called the "Teflon President," for blame never stuck to him. Atwater describes him:

> Reagan is not a power-hungry guy. Nixon was power hungry. Johnson was power hungry. Carter was power hungry. Look at the guys who were run out of town by the media—the guys who were obsessed with power. Reagan stays detached. He's got a Zen approach to power. He doesn't care about power for power's sake alone. Eisenhower is the only other person who had the same detached way of holding power.[12]

Reagan's success was based on his detachment from the power struggle.

Conclusion of Chapter 6:   Girard's theory of triangular desire and sacrifice describes social reality in a penetrating way. His theory teaches a very practical lesson, that is, the ability to discern the processes and patterns leading to mob violence and scapegoating. Once the theory is clear, the distinction between ethical behavior and mythical behavior should become clearer. Chapters seven through nine deal with practical approaches to ethical behavior within sacrificial systems.

Notes

1. Michael Lewis, *Liar's Poker: Rising Through the Wreckage on Wall Street* (New York: W. W. Norton, 1989) 185–6.

2. Peter Lynch, *One Up On Wall Street* (New York: Penguin Books, 1989) 43. Emphasis added.

3. Ibid., 61–2.

4. Donna Eder and Janey Lynne Enke, "The Structure of Gossip," *American Sociological Review* 56 (August 1991) 494.

5. See René Girard, *A Theater of Envy: William Shakespeare* (New York: Oxford University Press, 1991).

6. Peter Lynch, op. cit., 182.

7. Hedrick Smith, *The Power Game: How Washington Works* (London: William Collins, 1988) 82.

8. Robert Cialdini, *Influence: The Psychology of Persuasion* (New York: Quill, 1993) 128.

9. Ibid., 133.

10. Ibid., 145ff.

11. Hedrick Smith, op. cit., 57.

12. Ibid., 55.

CHAPTER 7

The Ethics of Survival: The Boss and the Mob

I don't want any yes-men around me. I want everyone to tell me the truth even if it costs them their jobs.

Samuel Goldwyn

At these words the whole audience was filled with indignation. They rose up and expelled him from the town, leading him to the brow of the hill on which it was built and intending to hurl him over the edge. But he went straight through their midst and walked away.

Luke 4:28-30

There are two kinds of people, those who do the work and those who take the credit. Try to be in the first group; there is less competition there.

Indira Gandhi

THE CONCEPT OF SURVIVAL

Self-protection: Survival is the art of self-protection. Because of the violence of mob behavior, survival depends on the ability to disappear from the attention of the mob. Furthermore, survival depends on maintaining a good relationship with the boss. Just as survival in jungle warfare uses camouflage, survival in the business world requires the art of invisibility. This art is acquired by practicing detachment from blame and credit or from the craving for recognition. People naturally want credit for what they accomplish, and resent blame for mistakes they did not make. This is basic justice. But the real world does not work this way.

Lessons from the Parables: If we deserve credit for the work we do, then how do we interpret the parable of the prodigal son (Luke 15:11-32)? In this parable the hardworking son is clearly more interested in recognition than a raise. And what happens? The lazy son is honored more than the hardworking son. Or how do we interpret the parable of the unjust steward (Luke 16:1-9)? The crafty steward is actually rewarded for being deceitful! How do we interpret the parable of the laborers in the vineyard (Matt 20:1-16)? How can it be fair or just that the people who work for one hour receive the same wage as the people who work all day? In all these parables no one receives the credit deserved. Is this ethical? No, not if we look at ethics only in the classical sense of distributive justice.

Street Smart Ethics: But if we look at business ethics in terms of an ethics of asceticism, then the parables begin to acquire new meaning. They teach us about radical detachment from blame and credit. They teach us more about social asceticism (mortification of the ego) than about physical asceticism (mortification of the body). Traditionally, people have read the Bible, especially the sayings of Jesus (e.g., the Sermon on the Mount and the parables) as a handbook containing a list of ethical precepts. Read this way, the parables present great difficulties for interpretation. What are the lessons we are supposed to learn from the parable of the unjust steward and the parable of the laborers in the vineyard?

Descriptive versus Prescriptive Ethics: Another possible way of approaching the parables is to read them as descriptive accounts of the way things are rather than as prescriptive accounts of the way things ought to be. When Jesus says that those who exalt themselves shall be humbled and those that humble themselves shall be exalted (Luke 14:11), he is not merely offering a prescriptive ethical rule—go out and practice conscious acts of humility. He is describing the context in which ethical struggles are played out. The way the world works is this—eventually, those who exalt themselves shall be humbled and those who humble themselves shall be exalted. The modern version of this paradox is: what goes around comes around. The parables, then, are street smart. They describe the way the world works. The lessons that we illustrate in the next three chapters can be read as modern parables.

A Modern Parable: Take for example one of those famous office memos that are faxed from office to office all over corporate America. These memos are always anonymous and mysteriously make the rounds. This particular memo is sometimes referred to as the Seven Phases of a Project. Sometimes it does not have a title. Sometimes only six phases are mentioned. It is a classic in the "oral tradition" of the business world.

The Seven Phases of a Project

1. Enthusiam
2. Illusion of Progress
3. Panic
4. Disillusionment
5. Search for the Guilty
6. Punishment of the Innocent
7. Praise & Honors for the Non-Participants

These seven phases perfectly describe the Management Complex. The seven stages describe the classic double-bind of employment: having accountability without having control.

The Message of Detachment: However, this parable teaches us that one way out of the double-bind is the acceptance of the inevitability of the double-bind. We are meant to laugh at it. This laughter is an ascetic discipline. Laughter teaches us detachment from office politics. The boss puts us in a double-bind. Someone else put the boss in one. Accept the inevitability of the seven phases. Avoid being trapped in the "search for the guilty" and the "punishment of the innocent" by becoming detached enough from the process to survive.

The Utility/Visibility Matrix: Of course, like the famous radio character of old, the Shadow, the art of invisibility entails both knowing how to disappear and how to reappear when it is useful. The art of invisibility must be learned before the art of visibility. Most people learn this lesson the hard way. They only study the art of invisibility after they have made a spectacle of themselves and have been scapegoated by the mob. One helpful device in learning protection from the mob is the Utility/Visibility Matrix. The chart's two main axes are the visibility axis and the utility axis. Everyone needs to examine whether their visibility is high or low and whether their utility is high or low.

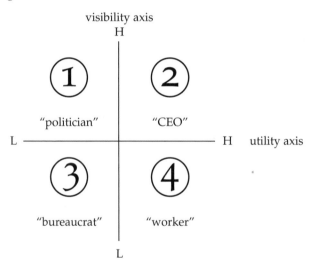

There are four possible quadrants:

Quadrant One: The quadrant of the politician is low utility and high visibility. It is the most precarious quadrant to be in. People can survive in this quadrant for years, but it is high risk for the individual and low return for the company. A company with a lot of quadrant one people is in the "too many chiefs and not enough Indians" quandary. If we were to categorize investments into the four quadrants, quadrant one would be that of the hot "initial public offering" with no earnings.

Quadrant Two: The quadrant of the CEO is high utility and high visibility. While more stable than quadrant one, two is much harder to achieve. The CEO must produce. By definition, very few people can achieve their niche in this quadrant. In terms of the stock market, quadrant two is where we find expensive growth stocks.

Quadrant Three: This is low utility, low visibility, the quadrant of the bureaucrat. A company with a lot of people in this category is in the "no pain, no gain" quandary. The federal government is a good example. In terms of the stock market, it is the quadrant of "widow and orphan" stocks.

Quadrant Four: This is high utility, low visibility, the quadrant of the worker, the quadrant where long-term survival and productivity are most assured. This is where we find the best "risk-adjusted" compensation for the work we do. In terms of stocks, it is the quadrant of value stocks, those that have good fundamentals but are out of favor in the market.

Peter Lynch's Rules: Lynch's rules for stock buying are descriptive of quadrant four.[1]

1. Buy a stock with a boring name (e.g., Automatic Data Processing).
2. Buy a stock that does something boring (e.g., Crown, Cork, and Seal makes bottle caps).
3. Buy a stock that is boring and disagreeable at the same time (e.g., Safety-Kleen makes machines that wash greasy auto parts).

In picking stocks, in picking employees, in picking careers, it is best to remember: "boring" can be a hidden asset. Value is found in low visibility and high utility. In the following section we will offer some practical tips on the art of invisibility. Some may work for you. Some may not. Take them with a grain of salt until they have proven themselves useful.

STRATEGIES IN SURVIVAL

Survival is underrated. Do not be embarrassed about setting your sites on survival. Just surviving office politics can be a heroic accomplishment by itself. Plenty of people do not even make it this far!

Keep your price-earnings ratio low. Price-earnings ratio (P/E) does not just refer to investment capital (the market price of a stock divided by its earnings per share). It also refers to political capital. What is the relation of your compensation (price) to your productivity (your company's earnings)? A high personal P/E is a symptom of high visibility relative to low utility. A low political P/E is a symptom of low visibility relative to high utility. In terms of survival, keeping a low P/E profile is the way to go.

Beware the compensation double-bind. Compensation is too often a function of visibility rather than utility. High visibility leads to high pay. But low visibility provides higher security. Make sure you know your goals before you grab for a higher paycheck.

Avoid the Peter Principle. The Peter Principle states that "in a hierarchy every employee tends to rise to his or her level of incompetence." Incompetence can be defined as the level where your visibility exceeds your utility. Your optimum survival niche should be where your visibility lags your utility by just a fraction.

Save political capital. People often produce best in the shadows of others. Learn to dwell in the shadows of others, sharing credit generously, and your "political capital" will gradually build. Do not be tempted to spend this capital. This is perhaps one of the lessons of the dishonest steward. "Use money, tainted as it is, to win yourselves friends, and thus make sure that when it fails you, they will welcome you into the tents of eternity" (Luke 16:9). Make friends by sharing your goods (i.e., your credit) with others.

Practice creative incompetence. A corollary of the Peter Principle states that too much competence or too little competence makes an employee a threat to the status quo of the office hierarchy. If your competence is making you too visible and a target of office jealousy, make mistakes that are socially embarrassing but do not reflect on your overall productivity. An occasional blunder in your dress or appearance works nicely. This provides justification for others' negative attitudes toward you and dissipates that negativity without threatening your overall position. Always give the adversary room to say "I told you so." Turn the other cheek a little. Frustrated negativity is more dangerous than satisfied negativity.

Blame and credit are two sides of the same coin.   You can not have one without the other. Social visibility results from your attachment to credit. It always carries the risk of becoming the scapegoat. It is not only a group's outcasts that are potential scapegoats, but also a group's idols. Both idols and outcasts live on the periphery of the group. As one newspaper columnist quipped after baseball star, Pete Rose, was convicted of illegal gambling: "The only thing Americans love more than an idol is a fallen idol."

The art of invisibility.   The best way to blend into the mob is to detach yourself from the cycle of blame and credit, while still closely observing its movements. If you are not detached, you draw attention to yourself by chasing credit and resisting blame. Resisting blame makes you stick out like a sore thumb. The mob senses your defensiveness and almost automatically circles in to teach you a lesson. If you continue to resist, your reputation can be permanently damaged. Craving credit has similar consequences. On the contrary, if you accept blame and relinquish credit in small ways, you remain invisible. Remember that all scapegoats start by being different.

Accept some dirty work.   Blame is a primal function of any job and avoiding it can be detrimental. Accepting blame can be part of your job security. It is another way of accepting the "dirty work" in a job. Blame is a hot potato; part of your job is to handle it. Where the "buck" (compensation) starts is where the "buck" (blame) stops. Job security is based on loyalty. Accepting blame for someone else tends to inspire loyalty.

Lose some battles.   Giving credit away is an important part of your job and not giving it away may cost you your job. Remember, blame follows credit. Credit is not always a good thing. You do not have to win every battle. It is easy to win battles and lose the war. John Lewis was the head of the United Mine Workers during World War II. He demanded a raise for the workers during the war (when wages were frozen), and his workers got the raise. The union as a whole lost credibility for being selfish during a time of crisis. And Lewis lost credibility.

The price of ambition is blindness.   Ambition and attachment to celebrity leads to tunnel vision and is therefore blinding. And celebrity exposes one to the whims of the mob. Like the prize fighter, the celebrity is both surrounded by the adoring crowd and his eyes are half shut from being beaten up.

The symbol of survival is the chameleon.   The chameleon is detached and observant. As the chameleon is detached from any specific color, you must be detached from any particular position or opinion. The chameleon is also very observant of its surroundings and therefore blends in perfectly. While being detached, you must follow the prevailing office politics with the utmost seriousness. Of course, the danger here is that nothing is worse than "bad camouflage."

You can not stick your head in the sand without exposing your rear flank.   The survival technique of the chameleon is not the survival technique of the ostrich. Do not stick your head in the sand. You can not be observant with your head in the sand. Furthermore, your utility will suffer, pushing you into quadrant three.

Institutionalize your eccentricities.   Whatever your eccentricities are, they cause you to stick out in the crowd. Maybe you are too good looking, too plain looking, too intellectual, too extroverted, too introverted, too obsessive-compulsive, etc.

Create a caricature of your own eccentricities for others instead of letting them do it behind your back. If you are defensive, you will be an easy target for unfavorable gossip. A sense of humor will automatically lessen the amount of attention that is focused on your foibles. Join in the gossip about yourself and you will defuse any serious scapegoating.

Office conflict is the result of a double hallucination.   In all office conflicts each party perceives the other person as a threat and retaliates accordingly. Retaliation reinforces the perception of a threat and a vicious cycle ensues. All insults are double hallucinations of the "insultor" and the "insultee" that are manufactured by the mimetic rivalry both people find themselves in. Remember—no one is really attacking you, only an image they have projected onto you.

Beware of insult by omission.   Your unintentional slights (ignoring someone) are more problematic than your intentional insults. Insults betray fear on the part of both parties. Most insults in the workplace are due to a perceived hiding of information ("why wasn't I invited to this meeting?" etc.).

Stay bland under pressure.   Do not lose your cool. Being bland under pressure signals a detachment from blame. This is a highly valued quality. Learn to be in the crowd without being of the crowd.

Do not get caught in the clash of Titans.   This results from trying to be visible—trying to get into the "inner circle." If you must communicate conflict between two bosses or employees, communicate the content without the emotion. Communicating the emotion puts you in the middle. Resist this temptation.

Make your boss look good.   The ultimate rule of survival is simple. Make your boss look good. Remember, your boss must do the same thing for his or her boss. It takes detachment and discipline to do this well. Assuming that your boss is relatively fair, you have a business-ethical obligation to reinforce his or her position and authority. Your respect helps create order in the system and can help bring out the best in your boss.

The cynicism of survival. Of course, making your boss look good can be taken to extreme. Consider Robert Jackall's fundamental rules of bureaucratic life in his study of corporate culture.[2]

1. You never go around your boss.
2. You tell your boss what he wants to hear, even when your boss claims that he wants dissenting views.
3. If your boss wants something dropped, you drop it.
4. You are sensitive to your boss's wishes so that you anticipate what he wants; you don't force him, in other words, to act as boss.
5. Your job is not to report something that your boss does not want reported, but rather to cover it up. You do what your job requires, and you keep your mouth shut.

In recounting the cynical truth of survival, Jackall describes how to be as shrewd as serpents, but not how to be as simple as doves. We are not encouraging managers to cover up the crimes of their bosses. Everyone must ask himself: at what point do I compromise my integrity in order to survive? We are, however, suggesting that managers learn to distinguish between corruption and humility.

The asceticism of survival. One positive thing the above rules teach us is not to take our own agenda so seriously. Much of what passes for self-righteous indignation in relationship to the boss is a mask for self-interest and resentment. The spiritual truth of the workplace is that the job will always disclose the secret attachments of your ego. The asceticism of survival teaches detachment from resentment and detachment from the double-bind. One way to solve the double-bind of the Management Complex is to pay close attention to the double-bind that your boss may be caught in. Another way to solve the double-bind of the Management Complex is to make your boss look successful. Live vicariously through your boss's success. That is your job and your spiritual path. The ethics of survival teaches you to resolve the double-bind as it expresses itself in relation to your boss. When you become detached from your boss as "model/obstacle," your boss disappears as a threat to your survival.

Notes

1. Peter Lynch, *One Up On Wall Street* (New York: Penguin Books, 1989) 122–4.

2. Robert Jackall, *Moral Mazes: The World of Corporate Managers* (New York: Oxford University Press, 1988) 109–10.

CHAPTER 8

The Ethics of Success: Competitors

If hard work made you rich, ants and peasants would rule the world.

Old Corporate Saying

Success is counted sweetest by those who ne'er succeeded.

Emily Dickinson

THE CONCEPT OF SUCCESS

From Survival to Success: The strategy of survival teaches detachment from an obsession with blame and credit. In doing so, this strategy teaches how to hide from the blame game. The strategy of success is trickier. This strategy challenges us to be political. It requires engagement in the blame game as well as the work of production. Success is based on the acceptance of the fact that there are two games going on in every business: the production game (which requires competence) and the blame game (which requires courage). To succeed, you must become proficient in both games. But before you begin to play, you must become aware of what you want. What is your definition of success? Success entails detachment from an obsession with survival (and fear of risk) as well as a detachment from an obsession with other people's successes. The trick is to focus on your success.

Winning and Gambling: The strategy of focus is different from the strategy of winning. We said at the beginning of this book that one of our primary goals is to help readers separate their productive selves from their competitive selves. This is accomplished by slowly separating from the seductive charms of borrowed desire. Borrowed desire operates according to the logic of gambling. The player obsessed with winning must constantly play for higher stakes. In a sense, the thrill of the game (and of desire) is this flirtation with disaster. The gambler courts disaster in the same way that the lover courts disaster and in the same way that the idolater courts disaster. The gambler toys with losing his or her money, the lover his or her heart, and the idolater his or her soul.

Means and Ends: If the object of desire were primary, the gambler would be more hesitant about losing the object of his love—money. But the gambler does not love money. The gambler loves the game. When the gambler wins a game, he must accept a greater challenge. When the seducer wins the heart of the beloved, he must seek out more resistant prey because he is in love with the game of seduction itself. "Winning" becomes pathological at precisely the instant it turns from a means into an end. When winning becomes an end in itself, the object of success disappears. Winning replaces producing.

The Art of the Deal: In the business world this idolatrous state also leads to the eclipse of the product and of the customer. When this thin line is crossed, a company begins a long slow march towards disaster. This phenomenon is seen very often in family businesses where sibling rivalry destroys a company from the inside because management is preoccupied by its internal power struggles. But it is also seen in competitive situations where product development suffers from an obsession with competitors.

Myths of Success: Pure competition is akin to religious fanaticism. This is why Calvinism and capitalism went so well together. However, in order to succeed we must temper our obsession with our model—whether that model be our boss, our competitor, our fellow employee, or even our deceased parent who started the business. Success requires detachment from success. Detachment from success requires "demythologizing" success. The mythological explanations that are given for success today are hard work, self-promotion, and ingenuity.

The Myth of Hard Work: The first explanation of success, the theory of hard work, is the easiest explanation to demythologize. Workers in underdeveloped countries often do back breaking work ten to twelve hours a day for a few dollars. They do this for their entire lives and never get rich. If hard work alone made people rich, these people would rule the world and they obviously do not. While hard work *might* be a necessary condition for success, it is definitely not enough by itself.

DILBERT reprinted by permission of United Features Syndicate, Inc.

The Myth of Self-Promotion: It is a cliche in certain business circles that the essence of success is the art of appearing successful ("fake it till you make it"). Girard describes this attitude well.

> Just think of all those manuals that claim to teach the secret of success, love, business, etc. What they reveal is always a strategy for relating to the other person. The one secret—the ideal recipe that is repeated over and over again—is that all you require for success is to give the impression that you have it already.[1]

Elsewhere, Girard describes this strategy of success as the narcissistic strategy of the coquette.

> The coquette knows a lot more about desire than Freud does. She knows very well that desire attracts desire. So, in order to

be desired, one must convince others that one desires oneself. That is how Freud defines narcissistic desire, as a desire of the self for the self. . . . The strategy of desire consists in setting up the dazzling illusion of a self-sufficiency that we shall believe in a little ourselves if we succeed in convincing the other person of it.[2]

Since the strategy of the coquette is rooted in the dangerous game of triangular desire, the outcome is tentative at best.

Self-Promotion: The self-promoter, like the gambler, is always tempted to play for higher stakes until he or she bets against a competitor that is more powerful. Stephen Covey has given a different, but equally persuasive, critique of this strategy which he calls the Personality Ethic. Covey alludes to borrowed desire in his critique of the Personality Ethic when he emphasizes the rule that "borrowing strength builds weakness."[3] Borrowing desire similarly builds weakness because it diffuses your focus and desire onto external factors.

The Myth of Ingenuity: The final myth about success is more difficult to analyze. Marketing professor, Steven Schnaars, has eloquently challenged the common assumption that innovation is a superior market strategy to imitation. Schnaars has analyzed dozens of cases in product development where later entrants into those markets gained significant market advantage over the original pioneers. He relates fascinating histories of everything from the development of 35mm cameras, ATM machines, and light beer to the pioneering of microwave ovens, money market funds, and software systems.

The Market Punishes Risk: In each case, the "first-mover" advantage of the pioneer is off-set by the "free-rider" advantages of the imitators. As Schnaars points out, the early pioneers of the American West took enormous risks to explore uncharted lands from which later settlers reaped the economic benefits.[4] Classic examples are products that were pioneered by Yankee ingenuity only to be undersold in the marketplace by low priced Japanese imitations. Small innovative companies often lose control of their inventions to larger competitors through the triple strategies of (1) lower pricing, (2) imitation *and* improvement, and (3) sheer market power (and the corresponding control of distribution networks).[5]

The Free-Rider Effect: For example, the pioneers of food processors (Cuisinart) and microwave ovens (Tappan) sold premium products at premium prices only to lose market share years later to imitators who sold lower-priced models of equal quality (Sunbeam and Samsung respectively). Later entrants did not have to absorb the expensive research and development costs of the pioneers. They could funnel their money into marketing. Early software pioneers (CP/M operating systems and Wordstar word processing systems) were clobbered by the improvements that later market entrants made to their products (Microsoft's MS-DOS and Word Perfect). The "first and worst" is often overpowered by the "second but better." Sheer market power took advantage of the pioneering efforts of smaller companies like Royal Crown (who created diet soft drinks) and Rheingold's Gablinger's (who created light beer) who lost market share to gigantic companies like Coke, Pepsi, Coors, and Budweiser.

Imitation or Ingenuity? Does Schnaars' analysis imply that we should abandon any efforts at ingenuity? We think not for three reasons. One, many successful imitators had to make innovations to existing products to gain market share. As Schnaars himself admits, innovation is often an incremental process with later market entrants having the advantage of greater innovation over the earlier market entrants.[6] Two, the individual imitator may be more successful financially than the pioneer, but the society as a whole is more successful because of the technological breakthroughs of the pioneer. If all companies emphasized marketing over research and development, the economy as a whole would stagnate. And three, newer computer technology may make the power of established distribution obsolete in the future. The Internet and other information access technologies may make direct order from the manufacturer routine someday. To quote Bill Gates:

> The Internet will extend the electronic marketplace and become the ultimate go-between, the universal middleman. Often the

> only humans involved in a transaction will be the actual buyer and seller. . . . On the network, lots of product information will be available directly from manufacturers.[7]

Pioneers might not lose their first entry advantage so quickly to those who control traditional, expensive distribution systems (the "middlemen") once computers create a world of automatic marketing and just-in-time inventory.

Whose Success?   The secret to success is overcoming the *craving for other peoples' successes.* The most common complaint we hear from individuals in business is that even in the moment of victory, there is a hollowness. No accomplishment, raise, promotion, or other milestone is ever quite enough. Without a disciplined working definition of "enough," we are forced to resort to comparisons in order to define "winning." We look for social confirmation to determine if we are winning. The problem is that no matter how much wealth, power, or achievement we have accumulated, there is always someone else around with more desirable accomplishments. If we continually succumbed to this borrowed standard of "enough," we would never succeed until the entire world, including God, finally stopped dead in its tracks and declared: "YOU HAVE EVERYTHING WE WANT!"

The Trick of Success: The trick of success is escaping the trap of striving to achieve what others declare valuable, and to answer for ourselves: "What do I want?" Without this step, we never achieve the focus that we need in order to perform effectively. Peter Drucker emphasizes that focus is the secret of results.

> Concentration is the key to economic results . . . no other principle of effectiveness is violated as constantly today as the basic principle of concentration. . . . Our motto seems to be: "Let's do a little bit of everything."[8]

The true measure of success, then, is achieving our own goals, not someone else's. Because desire tends to be so easily influenced by the desires of other people, setting and sticking to a personal set of goals is often the most difficult part of success.

STRATEGIES IN SUCCESS

Begin with an inventory.   Identify the categories of success in your life (personal, family, business, etc.). Write them down. Fill in your goals under each category. The point is to define victory. Do not leave anything out. In each of the above categories, what would you achieve if you had a magic wand? Literally. Beware the old adage: "Be careful what you wish for, you just might get it." If your goals are all financial, you may find yourself rich, divorced, and drinking too much.

First cut: revise your goals by a basic reality check. "Winning the lottery" is a valid goal for the magic wand step, but it gets cut at this stage. However, keep your magic wand list and set it aside for a rainy day—it has other uses.

Second cut: revise your goals by looking for internal contradictions.   This may be the most difficult part of the goal setting process. Not all of our dreams are realistically consistent with each other. The bad news in setting goals is that we must kill some of our dreams. The good news is that our dreams are more flexible than we think. In fact, disciplined goal setting is the only path to transforming our dreams from fantasies into realities. Until we accomplish this step, our dreams are the primary obstacles to our success. They are our enemies. Once transformed into goals, our dreams become the prime motivators of our success.

Third cut: negotiate with your key partners.   Start with the people in your life who matter the most. Obviously a spouse or a key business partner should not have fundamental objections to your goals. The more support you can gather, the less likely you are to being blown off course by borrowing others' desires. How many goals have been derailed by the age-old tragicomedy of adultery? Adultery is a classic example of borrowed desire undercutting the path to success. An astonishing percent of the time, the failure of key partners to "buy into" your personal goals is a contributing factor in these cases.

Last cut: fine tune your goals to reality (e.g., a timetable).   Take a few days to do this. Are you sure this is what you want? Remember the initial challenge of success is not getting what you want, but discovering what you want. Are you chasing anyone else's desire? It is okay to establish goals that are heavily influenced by other people so long as you are aware of those influences and adopt them with a clear awareness. Finally, now that you have your goals, stay focussed on them, but remain open to adjustments that are authentically your own.

Do not fixate on your boss as a model.   Imitation is the sincerest form of flattery and the deadliest. Do not imitate your boss, even if he or she encourages it. Your boss does not need a clone; your boss needs you. If you imitate your boss too successfully, you will make him or her nervous about being replaced by you. Your boss wants his/her ego fed, not replaced. Too often your performance suffers as you try to become someone that you are not. Again the movie *Wall Street* is instructive. Consider the following exchange at the end of the movie:

> Gordon Gekko: I look at you and I see myself. Why?
> Bud Fox: I don't know. I guess I realized I'm just Bud Fox. As much as I wanted to be Gordon Gekko, I'll always be Bud Fox.

Let your boss and co-workers know your dissimilarities. It is often useful to embrace caricatures of how different you are from your boss. Eccentricity, within boundaries, is good. Find your uniqueness and market those skills to your team. If you are the shortstop on the team, emphasize the fact that you play shortstop well, that you know your role, and that you are not trying to be a pitcher. The heart of productivity is the efficient division of labor.

**I shouldn't have to put up with this @&$%#!**   An important lesson to be learned in being successful is the overcoming of resentment. This is central to the development of what can only be called political maturity. You can survive and be resentful, but you cannot succeed and be resentful. Success requires finding contentment and a sense of joy in your job. A large obstacle to success is the very natural thought: "I shouldn't have to put up with this @&$%#!" The market may be an insane and irrational place. But because of this, it is the perfect place to learn the spiritual virtue of detachment, which is a necessary prelude to contentment. (Obviously there are some things that should not be tolerated. Detachment is very different from masochism. This distinction is a tough one.)

Beware of resentment. Resentment most often takes the form of the internal statement: "This place isn't fair because of politics." Of course the place is not fair! Fairness is not the nature of the game. However, politics is not an evil to be avoided, but a reality to be managed. ("It helps to know the difference between brick walls and speed bumps.")

I'm mad as hell and I'm not going to take it anymore. Remember the "liberated" news reporter in the movie, *Network?* He got everyone in the country to stick their heads out of their windows at home and scream: "I'm mad as hell and I'm not going to take it anymore." This statement is always a prelude to unemployment. The great thing about the job market is that it gives you unlimited opportunities to practice the virtue of detachment and to put up with unreasonable competitors, unreasonable bosses, unreasonable subordinates, unreasonable work loads, and unreasonable expectations. What a great learning environment!

When to question policy. It helps to question company policy when your audience is in a mood to listen. Or question policy when it is genuinely more important than the current timetable. Best of all, question policy when the questioning has been scheduled in advance and those most invested in the "status quo" have been given notice. This does not mean giving full advantage to opponents. Disarm opponents by addressing their objections honestly and credibly.

When in Rome do as the Romans. Engage in strategic temporary conformity. Do not overtly challenge the current cycle of blame and credit. Do not win battles that lose wars. Do not surrender to impulse in challenging the currency of blame and credit. Do not challenge everything that offends your values in the workplace. Impatience is usually driven by a false sense of urgency. Timing is everything.

When to execute policy. Execute policy when your audience is in a mood for results, not discussion. There is little benefit to screaming at deaf people. At times, we are all too deaf, too overwhelmed, or just too involved in something else that is currently more important.

When to follow stupid orders. Follow stupid orders when it is cheap to do so. A strategic flaw can often be exposed at little actual cost by small, well-executed, obedient mistakes. (The role of any level of management is to make sense out of the general orders pronounced by the level above it.)

When not to follow stupid orders. Do not follow stupid orders when it is expensive to do so or whenever someone could be seriously harmed.

Be "in" the office but not "of" the office. The office is a mythical system. You are part of the game and you cannot get out of it. But you are still responsible for how you act. Don't be morally self-righteous. You cannot deny the reality of office politics, but you can nudge it in certain positive directions. Remember, there is no such thing as a pure motive. But there is no such thing as a totally impure motive either.

Political problems are primary and technical problems are secondary. Information cannot flow properly until political tensions have been calmed. Focus on the political, and the technical obstacles will often take care of themselves.

Buy time to resolve conflicts by the "political/technical switch." If an office conflict is stuck in a rut, try altering the language that the conflict is articulated in. If the conflict is generally perceived as a technical problem, try to articulate it in political terms. If the conflict is generally perceived as a political problem, try to articulate it in technical terms. The mere change in language will often calm things down so that the problem can be approached more rationally. This approach does have limits. A premature switch in language can be misunderstood as a failure to understand "what's going on."

Success is always an ethical dilemma. Just as there are no markets without government, there is no power without politics. In order to succeed in any hierarchical structure, we must make peace with our desire to succeed. At the heart of this effort lies the central ethical problem: What am I willing to do to maintain my power? What am I unwilling to do to maintain my power? Our answers to these questions will determine our character and the sustainability of our success.

Do not use information as a weapon. Gossip is the ultimate inside information. Corporate raiders on Wall Street generate rumors to get the market moving in one direction and then exploit that movement by trading ahead of the market. Money is made, but nothing is produced. Gossip is the opposite of productivity. Gossip is information used as a weapon. It aggravates borrowed desire, jealousy, and rivalry. Productivity happens when information is used and shared as a tool. Success requires a willingness to risk and share information rather than hoarding it.

Compensation structures should reward, not punish the sharing of information across hierarchical lines. It is common for a supervisor to get paranoid when a subordinate goes out to lunch with the supervisor of another department or shares routine information without advance permission. Overcome the paranoia. Promote interdisciplinary communication among departments without permission being required. Employees' rewards should be based on the profits and values of the company as a whole, not on specific victories of any department by itself.

Information becomes valuable only when you give it away. Hoarding information leads to stagnation. Sharing information leads to productivity. Rather than manage a department's indispensability by hoarding knowledge, seek to manage obstacles to the sharing of information among departments. The world moves so fast in a technological age that the only way to stay on the curve is by sharing timely and quality information.

Success means headaches. The people that succeed and are content over the long run are the people that put up with constant headaches. They become detached from their resentment and begin to focus on their company's product and its customers. Everything else goes with the territory and is part of the job. Don't imagine that the successful people are the people without headaches. They are precisely the people that have assumed the most headaches and have accepted them.

The buggy whip phenomenon and mimetic blindness. All that glitters is not gold. Do not blindly imitate the competition or you end up with the classic buggy whip problem. (The buggy whip example is mentioned in Gordon Gekko's greed speech in *Wall Street* as well as most economics textbooks.) In the late 1800s, a particular company was the best buggy whip manufacturer in America. As cars began to replace buggies, their weaker competitors failed one after another. Finally only the strongest buggy whip maker survived. From a competitive analysis, they had one-hundred percent of the market and had beaten all their rivals. But they had market share in an obsolete market.

The double-bind is a way to control others, but a poor way to move ahead. The double-bind is a classic control technique. It keeps subordinates always off-guard and dependent on the model to solve the double-bind. Bureaucracies build the double-bind into their power structures by creating regulatory double-binds, e.g., obeying one rule to the letter of the law entails breaking another rule. This makes the worker dependent on the boss for a "solution" to the double-bind. This situation insures control, but destroys productivity. Work to dissolve double-binds. This is central to unlocking the creativity of your employees.

Love your enemies. Always channel your enemy's aggression back against the enemy so that each time the enemy is violent it becomes negative reinforcement. Your goal is not to beat your enemy, but to teach your enemy while remaining true to your own striving after excellence. Your goal is to convert not conquer the enemy. You do this by remaining in your own space and not being suckered out into mimetic conflict.

There are no enemies. The enemy is a mythical projection of your own aggression. Few opponents are worthy of being elevated to the status of "enemy." This is not to say that the effects of paranoia are not real. But the causes of paranoia are almost always exaggerated. There are no enemies, only paranoid projections.

The cynicism of success.   The cynicism of success is expressed in the old adage that winners must step on other people in order to succeed. Success may be perceived as a zero-sum game, but it need not always be at someone else's expense. People tend to believe that all successful people are cut-throat because they resent their success. Success in others is always resented by those without a clear idea of what they really want out of life. Remember, success is getting what *you* want, not chasing what others want. Resentment is not about what others have, but rather about who they are. They seem to be content. The true frustration is not that we lack what others have, but that we have not defined what we really want. Consider the example of the assembly-line workers and the foreman. In almost every such setting the foreman is resented on some level. This resentment becomes the prevailing ethic of the line workers. If a line worker is offered a promotion to foreman, he will experience this promotion as an ethical dilemma. The cynicism of success is that we must become what we hate in order to succeed.

The asceticism of success.   The ethics of survival teaches how to resolve the double-bind in relation to the boss. The ethics of success teaches how to resolve the double-bind ("be like me, don't be like me") in relation to competitors. The asceticism of success is to stick to your personal goals without becoming what you hate (without becoming like the model/obstacle). Your enemies multiply to the extent that you are not focused clearly on your own goals and are attracted mimetically to other people's goals. Focus on your goals and the number of your competitors will decrease. The only real competitor to your true self is your own ego. This is the only competitor you must defeat in order to succeed. Conventional wisdom teaches that once you have achieved success your competitors disappear. But the converse of that statement is a clearer path to success: once your competitors disappear, then you have achieved success. Loving your neighbor as yourself is a difficult precept to follow. In a mimetic environment, loving yourself as your neighbor is even more difficult. It is the true sign of success. The ethics of success teaches you to resolve the double-bind as it expresses itself in relation to your competitors. When you become detached from your competitors as "model/obstacles," your competitors disappear as obstacles to your success.

Notes

1. René Girard, THFW, 309.

2. Ibid., 370–1.

3. Steven Covey, *The Seven Habits of Highly Effective People: Restoring the Character Ethic* (New York: Simon & Schuster, 1989) 39.

4. Steven Schnaars, *Managing Imitation Strategies: How Later Entrants Seize Markets from Pioneers* (New York: Free Press, 1994) 15.

5. Ibid., 211.

6. Ibid., 198ff.

7. Bill Gates, *The Road Ahead* (New York: Penguin Books, 1995) 181–2.

8. Robert Townsend, *Up the Organization* (New York: Alfred Knopf, 1970) 130.

CHAPTER 9

The Ethics of Service: Customers

As for the best leaders, the people do not notice their existence. The next best, the people honor and praise. The next, the people fear; and the next, the people hate . . . When the best leader's work is done the people say, "We did it ourselves!"

Lao-Tzu

Leadership is an intangible quality with no clear definition. That's probably a good thing, because if the people being led knew the definition, they would hunt down their leaders and kill them.

Scott Adams

THE CONCEPT OF SERVICE

Customers as Turf: Borrowed desire always leads us to want what others have only because they have it and to defend what we have only because others want it. The first is a form of envy and the second is a form of jealousy. Much of strategic thinking consists of nothing more than resisting these impulses. If success requires that we resist these impulses when dealing with other people as competitors, service requires that we resist these impulses when dealing with other people as customers. The obstacle to service is the illusion that

107

our customers (both internal and external) belong to us. For example, the temptation to pander to "our" customers is a form of jealousy. The customer is always threatening to reduce our turf by going to a competitor. Our internal customers (e.g. our employees) might threaten to leave their jobs or to shift loyalties to another boss. Our external customers might threaten to take their business to a competitor. Many leaders succumb to this temptation to pander to customers' whims.

Leadership: The difference between merely pandering and true customer service is leadership. Leadership is always strategic by focusing on what customers really need rather than what they think they want. For example, Apple Computer jealously refused to license its operating system. John Scully pandered to one faction of his internal customers by giving them the hardware monopoly they thought they desired. If instead, Apple had freely licensed its operating system, Apple clones would have dropped in price as did PC clones. In that environment, Apple's superior operating system would have taken much greater market share. Scully failed to grasp what Bill Gates understood so well. Strategically giving away turf or credit for an idea or project (despite intense impulses to the contrary) almost always creates an advantage in a larger game.

Management versus Leadership: The primary concern of service is to meet the real needs, not the false desires of other people. This may involve "seducing" people into going where they need to go. Often this involves giving people credit for something you actually deserve. As Lao Tzu says: "When the best leader's work is done the people say, 'We did it ourselves!'" This is the heart of leadership—meeting others needs, often at the cost of allowing others to take the credit. It entails the overcoming of the craving to control. Control is a function of management, not leadership. Leadership seeks to inspire, not control. Service and leadership entail the belief that success is not a zero-sum game, but something that can be shared. Another modern parable that we have seen faxed around offices describes the distinction between management and leadership as follows:

Let's Get Rid of Management

People don't want to be managed.
They want to be led.
Whoever heard of a world manager?
World leader, yes.
Education leader.
Political leader.
Religious leader.
Scout leader.
Community leader.
Labor leader.
Business leader.
They lead.
They don't manage.
The carrot always wins over the stick.
Ask your horse.
You can lead your horse to water, but you can't manage him to drink.
If you want to manage somebody, manage yourself.
Do that well and you'll be ready to stop managing and start leading.

From Goals to Values: In the service dimension of our careers, we learn to make our talents useful to others and to detach ourselves from our goals and the self-images we have built around those goals. Even the most appropriate goals have a tendency to succumb to the craving to control. Success entails detaching from survival. Service entails detaching from success. The world is constantly changing. Our goals rarely keep up with the pace of change. Strategic flexibility requires transforming our goals into values. For example, in raising children we start off by wanting them to get straight "A"s or to grow up and become doctors. As reality intrudes on these inflexible goals, we learn that what we really want for them is integrity and happiness. This movement from goals to values allows us to become much more flexible in dealing with our children. The same is true for leadership in customer service. (After all, who is a tougher customer than your own kids?)

Jealousy and Envy: Jealousy leads us to pander to our customers. Envy leads us to dictate to our customers. When we dictate ultimatums to our employees, we envy them their freedom from our control. The impulse of borrowed desire is to want what someone else has only because they have it. Our need to control often stems from our envy of other people's freedom. Just as the difference between pandering and service is leadership, so also the difference between dictating and service is leadership. For example, consider the story of Tom Sawyer and the fence. Tom had a job that had been dictated to him. He had to whitewash a very long fence while his friends were out enjoying the day. When one of those friends came along, Tom pretended as if fence painting was so fulfilling and fun that he barely had time to talk. Before long, the whole town was lined up to pay Tom for a turn at painting the fence. The fence got three coats, Tom got rich and barely lifted a finger in the process. Tom's fence story is a perfect model for leaders. Tom took "gruntwork" and transformed it into something so desirable that his "employees" were paying for the chance to work. For those who painted the fence, he had created meaningful employment. No one walked away from the fence with quite the same vision of fence painting that he had beforehand.

Internal Customer Service: Tom treated his workers as true "customers" and creatively gave them what they needed, not what they thought they wanted. This kind of internal customer service is what true leadership is all about. When you realize that everyone is a potential customer, all strategy becomes a question of customer service—service to employees, service to stockholders, service to peers, service to those who purchase and use our products. Rather than despairing of his goal of playing all day, Tom transformed the burden of fence painting into a game. By detaching from his rigid goal of going fishing, he discovered one of his core values (which was simply to play). By focusing on the value of play rather than on his goal of fishing, Tom accomplished his task without either pandering or dictating terms to his associates.

External Customer Service: All businesses try to build superior external customer service. Without a grasp of the basic values that define a company, customer service is impossible. Without service, there is nothing to sell. Davidow and Uttal in *Total Customer Service* describe customer service as the "ultimate weapon."

> Because a successful customer service program affects every person in every part of your business, driving to improve service means nothing less than driving to transform your corporation from top to bottom. Is it worth it? . . . The benefits of producing superior customer service, we believe, far outweigh the costs, and so do the penalties of delivering shoddy service. Besides, there's no choice. In the long term, service leaders destroy service followers. The only course for managers interested in survival is to forge and master the ultimate weapon.[1]

Both external and internal customer service have the same challenge. The difference between leadership and management, both in external and internal markets, is a service approach. Both customers and employees resent being managed and respond to being led.

CALVIN AND HOBBES © Watterson. Dist. by UNIVERSAL PRESS SYNDICATE. Reprinted with permission. All rights reserved.

The Ethical Dilemma of Service: The ethics of service is not rule-bound, but value-laden. The ethical dilemma of service is where to draw the line in exploiting the knowledge of mimetic desire to produce good results. This is precisely the ethical trade-off that Tom Sawyer must face. He uses his instinctive knowledge of borrowed desire to make a task worth doing. Obviously this is a treacherous path. The temptations to consciously manipulate other people "for their own good" or "for the greater good" (or just to increase productivity) are immense. But Tom's episode demonstrates that good things can come even from the blatant manipulation of another's envy (at least in the short run). All "service" approaches are prone to the temptation of imposing our own values on others in the name of altruism.

Ethical Solution: One solution may be to define service as providing others with what they need to be free. This notion of service as the creation of liberty can influence every aspect of our business lives. Our products and services should provide what people need to be more free. The use of celebrity models who whip up markets into frenzies of envy can literally be carried to such extremes that kids get shot over a pair of sneakers or a professional sports jacket. On the other hand, the very same celebrity advertising techniques can promote auto sales, providing useful products and thousands of new jobs.

The Empowerment Debate: Service, that is, the creation of liberty, puts us in the middle of the great "empowerment" debate. The failure of empowerment in most office settings is caused by managers who are inattentive to the details of what their employees need in order to be free. One thing they always need are clear limits. Just as markets cannot be truly free with too much or too little government intervention, employees cannot be free without a clear understanding of the limits and the scope of their freedom. Without this understanding, fear of being labelled "insubordinate" will kill empowerment. How can I harness my creativity to solve a puzzle that confronts me on the job without running to the boss for guidance, unless I know the rules of the game? Empowerment can be killed either by pandering or by dictating.

Service and Cost Control: An ethic of service also drives cost control. Budget disciplines are simply the ultimate backbone to empowerment. As a former CEO of Avis says:

> A tight budget brings out the best creative instincts in man. Give him unlimited funds and he won't come up with the best way to a result. Man is a complicated animal. He only simplifies under pressure. He'll scream in anguish. Then he'll come

up with a plan which, to his own private amazement, is not only less expensive, but also faster and better than his original proposal.[2]

The budget is a crucial limit on the scope of freedom. It is a fundamental rule of the game. It should be negotiated with the highest levels of creative thinking about who we are and where we are headed. Rules for budget negotiations should be crystal clear. The purpose of the budget is to set us free. Once established, it allows our talent to focus. The budget and business plan, if done correctly, unlock the talent base of our organization.

Free Markets: Ultimately, the market can be free: not free from basic government regulation, not free from management's limits and controls, not free from budgets, not free from responsible marketing, but free within those limits and free from borrowed desire. And, we should add, free to create value. The purpose of the ethic of service is precisely to create free markets by freeing the people within them to apply their talents in full participation in the economic life of the community.

Strategies in Service

Values inventory.   The essence of our values is located in our relationship with others: our families, friends, communities, and co-workers. As we move along our career paths, seeking to avoid borrowing other peoples' desires and goals, we eventually learn to focus on who we are. At this stage, an inventory of our relationships and our talents will lead us to discover the basic values that we hold.

Relationship list.   First, make a list of all key relationships in your life—and do not categorize them. Allow family and business to jumble together. Relationships have their own logic.

Talent list.   Second, make a list of personal strengths and weaknesses. This is the time for ruthless honesty. Without putting everything on the table, you are sure to be blindsided by the things you deny. Ask other people.

Comparison of lists.   Third, apply the talent list to the relationships list. How do these two lists match up? Take an inventory of which of your talents and skills are being used in which relationships.

Evaluation.   Fourth, evaluate whether these matchings are satisfactory or not. Do not become goal-oriented here. Do not ask "what do I want to do?" but "who do I want to be?"

Values statement.   Fifth, with a blank sheet of paper and some serious quiet time, draft a written description of your basic values. Who do you want to become in the specific context of your key relationships?

The stage of service.   You are now at the stage of service. Service is what you are doing when you are not borrowing desires and chasing the appealing appearances of other peoples' lives. Service is simply the application of your strengths and weaknesses in relation to others, and service should be at the heart of your workplace strategies.

The Tom Sawyer composting technique.   Make the boring, mundane tasks of the workplace attractive. After all, real productivity is in sweating the details, not in the glamour of "management." One way to do this is for leadership to periodically get its hands dirty and pitch in on unpleasant tasks. Even more important is for leadership to unlock the creative freedom of a team's talent despite the appearance of a mundane or boring task.

Gruntwork as alienating/gruntwork as liberating.   Is secretarial work more dehumanizing than managerial work? Does the relative pay that each of the two receives make a difference? Or just less socially desirable? Is Michelangelo's painting of the Sistine Chapel more or less dehumanizing than Tom Sawyer's friends' painting Aunt Polly's fence? Is an auto worker's labor on an assembly line more or less dehumanizing than a monk's baking hundreds of loaves of bread? Does their attitude make a difference?

The Becky Thatcher technique.   Another of Tom Sawyer's techniques was taking blame strategically. Remember in the novel when Becky Thatcher was looking at a picture in the teacher's anatomy book and accidentally ripped a page. The teacher found out and asked who ripped the book. In order to win Becky over, Tom took the blame for it and was punished severely by the teacher. "But when he stepped forward to go to his punishment, the surprise, the gratitude, the adoration that shone upon him out of poor Becky's eyes seemed pay enough for a hundred floggings" (Mark Twain's *Tom Sawyer*). Try this technique the next time you want to gain a little political capital with your boss or peers.

Scapegoat concepts, not people.   If you are stuck with a problem that won't go away, trying blaming the problem on something impersonal like "a lack of communication" or a "confused process." Create a "safe triangle" with a concept as the third leg of the victimage triangle. Everyone saves face with this excuse, so it is another good way to lower levels of tension, giving everyone time to solve the problem in a rational way.

If it ain't broke, don't fix it.   Don't find problems to fit your MBA solutions. Such good intentions are the kind that pave the way to hell. Politicians manufacture problems in order to gain visibility and get elected.

Follow the value theory of hiring.   Look for undervalued people in your company. Educating, delegating, and giving responsibility to these people produces the greatest return. Respect an employee's lack of desire for the limelight.

Hire people in teams.   People that work well together should be hired in pairs or groups. Think about hiring teams instead of hiring individuals. Effective teams have often already worked out their politics in healthy and successful ways. Henry Ford pursued this strategy at the end of World War II when he hired a group of ten officers from the Air Force who wanted to continue working as a team in the private sector. Robert McNamara and the famous Whiz Kids turned "his grandfather's huge but ailing company" around.[3] (History has proven they should have stayed at Ford.)

Respect the autonomy of healthy teams.   In any given business, different departments have different cultures and different ways of operating. Accounting departments tend toward a military style chain of command and respect for procedure. Marketing departments tend to value relationships and loyalty more than rigid procedures, preferring to view rules as "guidelines." Legal departments tend to allow even last minute analysis on any topic or policy. These stylistic differences tend to create what could be called "ethnic conflicts" in the workplace. Departmental rivalry comes from focusing on other departments instead of your own. Do not strive for their success or do not borrow their methods. Find a common language with which to bridge the culture gap.

The Good Samaritan technique.   Sacrificial managers automatically shun their subordinates when these subordinates end up in trouble. They fear being "contaminated" by a subordinate who is in danger of being scapegoated. But this fear of contamination is a double-edged sword. Unless you are willing to risk your neck for your subordinates and stand up for them, you can be sure they will never take risks for you. The violence of a sacrifice in the workplace is in direct proportion to the status of the person being sacrificed. The righteous wrath of the mob is stronger towards those lower on the totem pole. A manager who has more political capital than his or her subordinate can take a hit more easily than the subordinate. By taking the blame for a subordinate, the manager lessens the amount of violence in the workplace and gains a powerful ally in the subordinate. This is the technique of "strategic surrender." This technique is used when a productive subordinate's political capital would be unfairly destroyed by taking the blame and the boss's would only be dented. (Of course, this technique should not be used blindly to cover up a subordinate's serious incompetence.)

The "second-person" technique.   In her studies of adolescent gossip, sociologist Donna Eder has observed that "the first response to an initial evaluation in a gossip episode strongly influences subsequent responses."[4] Adolescents feel comfortable challenging the negative remarks by an individual, but not by a group. Therefore, the second remark in a gossip episode is crucial. If the second remark challenges the initial denunciation, other negative remarks tend to die off. If the second remark confirms the original denunciation, the group circles in for the kill and the other negative remarks about the absent victim are almost impossible to stop. Ironically, Eder notes that "responses by even low-status group members can have considerable influence on the course a gossip episode takes."[5] This second-response technique can be an invaluable tool in lessening sacrificial movements in the workplace.

Build trust by being loyal to those not present. Resisting the temptation to gossip is a strong method of building trust in an organization. As Stephen Covey says: "One of the most important ways to manifest integrity is to *be loyal to those who are not present*. In doing so, we build the trust of those who are present. When you defend those who are absent, you retain the trust of those present."[6]

Vote neither Republican or Democrat. As the ex-mayor of New York, Fiorello LaGuardia once said, "There's no such thing as a Democratic or Republican way to collect the trash." Politics slow up the process of getting the job done. The Democrat is trapped by envy and mimetic desire. The Democratic mob screams about "rights." The Republican is trapped by sacrifice and violence. The Republican crowd screams about "law and order." Focus on customer service. Focus on the garbage.

The customer double-bind. The customer double-bind can be expressed in two platitudes. One, as Thomas J. Watson, Jr. said: "IBM means service." This is often translated as "the customer is king" or "the customer is always right." Two, as P. T. Barnum said: "there's a sucker born every minute." Michael Lewis translated P. T. Barnum's remark into the modern investment world when he overheard one of Salomon's seasoned bond traders remark to a naive trainee, "You are proof that some people are born to be customers."[7] Whose advice do we take, Thomas J. Watson, Jr.'s or P. T. Barnum's? The exchange between business and customer resembles the sacrificial exchange between humans and the gods that we discussed in Chapter 5: *du ut des.* "I give so that you will give in return." Which offering is primary? The business's product to the customer? Or the customer's payment to the business? Does the business exist to serve the customer? Or does the customer exist to serve the business? Every business transaction has this tension built into it.

The cynicism of service. Whichever philosophy you choose, every customer wants all of your attention. Every customer wants more of you than you can afford to give. But this is impossible! The customer thinks as follows: "I'm the customer. I have problems and needs. As far as I'm concerned my problems are the only problems in the world. Good customer service means I want you to be like me by getting into my shoes and making my problems your only problems. But I don't want you to be completely be like me because I don't want to solve my own problems. That's your job!" Just as in all the other binds, if you give everything to one customer you will go out of business and you won't solve anyone's problems. You must balance one customer's needs with another customer's needs in order to stay in business and satisfy anyone. The double-bind in customer service is summarized in Aesop's fable: "please all and you please none."

The asceticism of service. The way to eliminate cynicism is by detaching from false idealism. The "customer is always right" is an example of a well intentioned but false idealism. What if the customer is Adolf Hitler and wants parts for his ovens? What if the customer demands child pornography? Or, take the everyday dilemma faced by Certified Public Accounting firms. The double-bind here is particularly harsh. The customer pays the CPA firm to police the operations of the customer! Does the CPA firm overlook certain improprieties in order to keep the account? Or does the CPA firm tell the truth and risk losing the account? Honest customer service sometimes entails not satisfying the customer. The ascetical discipline needed in order to provide real customer service is humility. Don't lie to the customer. Don't make false promises.

Don't pretend to be able to deliver what you can't. You can't please all customers. And the customers know this. But you can please some. And this is the task. What this spiritual discipline boils down to is niche marketing. Figure out what you are good at and do it.

Notes

1. William Davidow and Bro Uttal, *Total Customer Service* (New York: Harper and Row, 1989) 217.

2. Robert Townsend, *Up the Organization* (New York: Alfred Knopf, 1970) 187.

3. Lee Iacocca, *Iacocca: An Autobiography* (New York: Bantam Books, 1984) 41.

4. Donna Eder and Janey Lynne Enke, "The Structure of Gossip," *American Sociological Review* 56 (August 1991) 495.

5. Ibid., 495.

6. Stephen Covey, *The Seven Habits of Highly Effective People: Restoring the Character Ethic* (New York: Simon & Schuster, 1989) 196.

7. Michael Lewis, *Liar's Poker: Rising Through the Wreckage on Wall Street* (New York: W. W. Norton, 1989) 171.

CHAPTER 10

The Wisdom of Tradition: Work

Before enlightenment, chopping wood and hauling water.
After enlightenment, chopping wood and hauling water.

Zen proverb

There can be no joy in life if there is no joy in one's work.

Thomas Aquinas

Just do it.

Nike ad

Traditional Ethics? We all need to integrate our individual ethics within the wisdom of our own religious or philosophical traditions. The tradition of the authors is Catholicism. We understand that some elements of our tradition may be alien or even offensive to some of our readers. Nonetheless we encourage you to consider this last chapter on its own terms and to make the effort required to translate the tradition and wisdom of someone else into your own. Again, we believe that ethics is essentially experimental. Living out the wisdom of any tradition requires trial and error. In this final chapter we attempt to locate our thesis within our own tradition of Catholic social teaching. We do so in a spirit of intellectual honesty. Take it for what it is worth.

Catholic Social Teaching: Catholic social teaching emphasizes a balance between the desire for success and a respect for others. It is possible to be ethical and successful at the same time. But true success is not borrowed in envy by looking over your neighbor's fence. Our purpose is not to show how Jesus can make you rich. If Jesus came to make us rich, he set a singularly poor example of how to do it. Nor is our purpose to show how Jesus can make you poor. Jesus never turned poverty into an idol. He consorted with tax collectors and rich people as well as with peasants. Once again, if Jesus was a revolutionary he left a poor blueprint for political transformation. The three-part structure of our practical ethics (survival, success, and service) mirrors the U.S. Bishops' pastoral letter on economics:

> All work has a threefold moral significance. First, it is a principal way that people exercise the distinctive human capacity for self-expression and self-realization. Second, it is the ordinary way for human beings to fulfill their material needs. Finally, work enables people to contribute to the well-being of the larger community. Work is not only for one's self. It is for one's family, for the nation, and indeed for the benefit of the entire human family.[1]

Survival, successful self-expression, and service—each of these three aspects of work has its own distinct moral character.

Struggle for Survival: The struggle for survival is based upon our desire for security. Our most primitive impulses on the job arise from our insecurities about material needs, i.e., putting bread on the table. However, these anxieties quickly go beyond material concerns and develop a social focus. Will the boss fire me today? What do I need to do to please the boss? Worrying about putting bread on the table readily shifts into worrying about kissing our boss's posterior anatomy. The ethics of survival typically involves a conflict between obedience to our "boss" and obedience to our values. Common examples include being sexually harassed, being ordered to lie, or being expected to work at a time promised to family. There is a positive side to survival and a dark side to survival. Survival puts us in a double-bind. How far are we willing to stretch our integrity in order to survive? Without our integrity, who is it that survives?

Struggle for Success: The struggle for success is based upon the desire to achieve certain goals and aspirations. Work is a form of self-expression or self-realization. We are what we do (or at least we become so). The ethics of success involves the conflict between defeating our rivals and protecting our values. Competing with others for a raise is the perfect example. When in survival mode, our obsession is with security. When in success mode, our obsession is with winning. Like survival, the success mode has a positive and a dark side. The positive side to success is creative and even playful self-expression. The dark side is obsessive competition in which our rival's self-expression eclipses our own.

Struggle for Service: The struggle to provide service is based upon the desire to contribute to something outside ourselves. Work is a contribution to the common good. The ethics of service involves the conflict between meeting the needs of our "customer" and preserving our own values. Prostitution is the ultimate metaphor for the double-bind of customer service. The artist asks, "am I prostituting myself to make my work commercial?" The charity seeking donations asks, "are we prostituting ourselves in taking a large donation from a known spouse abuser?" The multi-national manufacturer asks, "are we prostituting ourselves by supplying equipment to Chinese toy factories?"

The Three Modes: These modes of survival, success, and service are not necessarily sequential. Like moods, our modes can change every fifteen minutes during the workday. At the same time each person—or even each business—tends to have a dominant mode at any point in its life cycle, and this dominant mode can evolve and change over time. This distinction between survival, success, and service is reminiscent of a distinction made by Thomas Aquinas in his discussion of natural law.[2] Since humans are created by a good and loving God, there is a goodness in their natural inclinations. The three primary natural inclinations are: (1) self-preservation, (2) procreation and the education of children, and (3) life in society and a knowledge of truth. First, human beings seek the preservation of their own being. Second, human beings have an innate desire to reproduce the most personal dimensions of their selves. And third, human beings, as rational animals, desire to know the ultimate truth and to contribute to the common good. The first and third inclinations bear close resemblance to survival and service. The second inclination, to reproduce one's self, is intimately tied to the drive for success. Whether literally as in the conception and parenting of one's offspring, or figuratively as in "giving birth" to a business or career (or juggling both!), success is a form of self-expression. Success in business or in parenting or in the arts and sciences is ultimately a reflection of the deep longing to "leave our mark" on the world.

Micro Ethics: In the field of business ethics, recent Catholic social teaching has tended to focus on macro issues at the expense of micro issues. For example, the U.S. Bishops' economics pastoral offered a cogent and necessary critique of sinful economic structures and proposed various economic reforms. What is often lost in this macro analysis of sinful structures are the moral dilemmas facing individuals in their daily work lives.

Structure and Myth: An understanding of the mechanism of scapegoating provides an important contribution to this "structural" understanding of sin. We tend to deny the ugly reality of scapegoating and to mythologize the political and economic structures which require it. Each new structure tends to be founded on a new vision of "us" and "them." The installment of a new structure tends to include the expulsion of those who symbolize "them." (With typical drama, Girard argues that each new culture requires a "founding murder.") All of this leads to a healthy skepticism about the extent to which unjust structures can be toppled overnight and replaced by just structures. The fall of the Berlin Wall has hardly been replaced by the Garden of Eden in the former Soviet bloc.

Sinful Structures: Our approach to micro business ethics might be considered a radical extension of Catholic social teaching in analyzing the structure of sin. Modern capitalism was born of the utopian dream that society's ethical problems could be solved at the structural level. The rough competition of a free marketplace would miraculously transform the private vice of greed into the public virtue of prosperity. Similarly, Communism was born of the utopian dream that society has the potential to treat each person with perfect fairness if only we can replace the unjust structures that make us behave badly. Change the unjust structures and human nature itself will change for the better.

Economic Structures: Neither of these new economic structures has been particularly successful at realizing a utopian vision of peace, harmony, and universal prosperity. The fact that this book focuses on the myths of the capitalist marketplace is not an indication of communist sympathies. Capitalism has proven itself to be less brutal than its communist alternative. However, the business world in which we all live *is* capitalistic, and the existence of greater evils should not distract us from the ethical issues within our own economic system. Our pragmatic concern must be to examine ways in which each of us can act ethically within actual social structures that are far from perfect. Specifically, how can we responsibly manage the daily struggles of our business world in all of its ethical complexity? We are not always helped in this struggle by our utopian dreams or the myths that we create to keep those dreams alive. For this reason we focus on the role of mythology in the capitalist business world.

The Market as Myth: The market is littered with the laurels of its victors and the corpses of its victims. The myth of the free market legitimizes the winnings of the victors and the losses of the victims. If the government is the referee in business, then the market is the scorekeeper. As final arbitrator of success and failure, the market is god. Within this system the Federal Reserve Bank functions as one of many high priests, balancing the threat of inflation with the threat of unemployment—sacrificing job creation on the altar of long-term economic growth. To the layperson, the ways of the market and its priests have become too complex to second guess. In the face of mystery, the prevailing myth of the free market urges us to have "faith" in its inscrutable judgments.

Macro versus Micro Business Ethics: A complete macro ethical critique of the free market lies beyond the scope of this book. This does not imply that the issues of unemployment, downsizing, or corporate responsibility are unimportant. They are. However, micro business ethics focuses on how the individual functions ethically within existing structures. The unfairness inherent in any market mechanism provides each individual and each company with an opportunity for ascetical practice and ethical behavior. The challenge of macro business ethics is the balance of the equitable distribution of goods and services with an adequate reward system that encourages incentive. The challenge of micro business ethics is to transform mythical behavior into ethical behavior. The purpose of Chapters 7 through 9 has been to encourage the reader to be less competitive and therefore more productive and more ethical.

Work as Punishment: As we said in Chapter 1, the monastic tradition regards work as an ascetic discipline. This ascetic discipline has generally been interpreted in two different ways—asceticism as punishment and asceticism as therapy. Work likewise can be viewed as punishment or as therapy. For many centuries the discipline of work was viewed as a punishment for the sin of Adam and Eve. Work was viewed as a way to atone for sin. Many scholars trace the origin of this punitive view of work to Irish monasticism, what might be called "quid pro quo" asceticism.[3] Work is fundamentally an economic transaction, a repayment of our debt to God due to our sins. Work is just one form of payment within this sacrificial system. Other forms include fasting, celibacy, silence, sleep deprivation, and seclusion. (Sound like *your* job?) The monks who could handle this kind of discipline were viewed as professional Christians. This view of work as punishment is still popular today.

Reprinted with the permission of the publishers of *Crisis: Politics, Culture and the Church,* 1814¹/₂ N Street N.W., Washington, D.C. 20036.

Work as Therapy: Other monastic traditions, however, interpreted asceticism as a form of healing or therapy. As we stated earlier, the origin of the Greek *askesis* comes from the world of sports and carries no negative connotations. It simply means practice or training. Asceticism refers to the rigorous training that an athlete endures. Early Christians took over this sports metaphor and developed the notion of the "spiritual athlete." The saints were people who were proficient in Christian virtue. As St. Paul says: "Every athlete exercises discipline in every way. They do it to win a perishable crown, but we an imperishable one" (1 Cor 9:25). Early Christianity saw work as a healing of sin rather than a punishment for sin. Interestingly enough, the Greek word *therapeia*, from which we derive our word "therapy," has many connotations to the world of work. Definitions of *therapeia* include service to others, medical attention to the sick, cultivation of the land, as well as general maintenance, i.e. "to take care of" (Liddell & Scott). The Greek root of therapy implies the simple notion of tending to one's chores and being of service to others. The conclusion is simple: service to others is therapeutic. John Paul II goes beyond the view of work as therapeutic to emphasize work as a blessing. As one of the many commentators on John Paul II's *Laborem Exercens* states: "Work is not a curse, it is a blessing from God who calls man to rule the earth and transform it, so that the divine work of creation may continue with man's intelligence and effort."[4]

The God Complex: We argue that the purpose of work is not only to transform the earth, but to transform ourselves. Work is therapeutic in that it continually forces us to confront and resolve our double bind. The world of work (much more than the world of prayer or the world of study) forces us to confront our frustrated desire. This frustration plays itself out in business life as the Management Complex. The world of work forces us to face our limitations and our fundamental stance toward authority, whether that authority wears the face of boss, rival, or customer. It is precisely in the world of work that we work out our fundamental double-bind (that we are both like and unlike God). In his encyclical on human labor, *Laborem Excercens,* John Paul II analyses work as the imitation of God:

> The description of creation, which we find in the very first chapter of the Book of Genesis, is also in a sense the first "gospel of work." For it shows what the dignity of work consists of: It teaches that man ought to imitate God, his creator, in working, because man alone has the unique characteristic of likeness to God.[5]

Through work, we become "co-creators" with God. God "works" in order to create the world (Gen 2:2). But the very term "co-creator" implies a double-bind. As John Paul II reminds us, we share in the "activity of the Creator" but "within the limits of our own human capabilities." In work we realize our creative potential as well as our inherent limitations. Even the struggle of manual labor exerting itself against the inertia of nature is a spiritually purifying struggle. Likewise, in the world of office politics, the struggle of management exerting itself against the inertia of bureaucracy is a spiritually purifying struggle.

The Double-Bind and Entrepreneurship: Building businesses in our dreams is much different than building businesses within the reality of shifting market conditions. Without the dream, there would be no business. As Anatole France put it: "Without dreamers, mankind would still live in caves." Every successful business is started by someone who dares to dream and to be creative. However, every successful business survives because of someone who pays close attention to the financial limitations within the business.

Genesis Revisited: John Paul II emphasizes that work makes us more human. In transforming nature to meet our needs we experience God working within us. Several times in *Laborem Exercens* John Paul stresses the divine command for human beings to subdue the earth. The first chapters of Genesis make clear that work is not merely a curse. The command to work is made at least twice before the Fall of Adam. In the first account of creation, after man and woman are created "in the likeness" of God, they are encouraged to "be fruitful, multiply, fill the earth and conquer it" (Gen 1:28). In the second account of creation, after Adam is placed in the garden, he is expected to work. "God took the man and settled him in the garden of Eden to cultivate and take care of it" (Gen 2:15). However, this notion of work as a blessing is balanced by the punitive aspects of work that are described after the Fall.

> Accursed be the soil because of you. With suffering shall you get your food from it every day of your life. It shall yield you brambles and thistles, and you shall eat wild plants. With sweat on your brow shall you eat your bead, until you return to the soil, as you were taken from it. (Gen 3:17-19)

Here again we see the double-bind. Be like God (work as creative). Don't be like God (work as curse). It should be noted that work only acquires its painful aspect after Adam and Eve follow the serpent's suggestion that they can be like God in all things. Their attempt to be like the boss leads to their eventual demotion.

Experimental Ethics: The resolution of the Management Complex is by nature experimental. The micro ethics we propose is based on experience. Everyone must resolve the complex in his or her own way based on his or her own experience. What works for one person may prove disastrous for another. *Caveat emptor!*

The Management Complex: We have set forth the basic principles of the Management Complex and proposed possible ways to transform mythical behavior into ethical behavior. In doing so, individuals can avoid spiritual as well as financial bankruptcy. Hopefully, by outlining the principles of virtuous business from a micro perspective, we might enable individuals to bring a modicum of freedom into the unfree marketplace of imitation and sacrifice.

Free Markets: The ideal of a free market should not be to free the market, but to free the people within the market. We become free from borrowed desire, from envy, from mindless competition to the extent that we stop trying to escape the simple, mundane effort of everyday labor. Workplace politics is what we invent to avoid gruntwork. The entire business hierarchy is designed to define some work as more prestigious and self-fulfilling than other work. The fact is that work is the universal path to enlightenment for all workers, no matter how unimaginative or routine the job may seem. As the Zen proverb has it:

> Before enlightenment, chopping wood and hauling water.
> After enlightenment, chopping wood and hauling water.

Notes

1. National Conference of Catholic Bishops. *Economic Justice for All: Pastoral Letter on Catholic Social Teaching and the U.S. Economy* (Washington D.C.: United States Catholic Conference, 1986) 50.

2. Thomas Aquinas, *Summa Theologica* I-II, Q. 94, a. 2.

3. Michael Downey, ed., *The New Dictionary of Catholic Spirituality* (Collegeville: The Liturgical Press, 1993) 64.

4. Al Gini, "Meaningful Work and the Rights of the Worker: A Commentary on *Rerum Novarum* and *Laborem Exercens*," *Thought* 66 (September 1992) 229.

5. Pope John Paul II, "*Laborem Exercens*," *Origins* 11, no. 15 (September 24, 1981) 241.

Questions for Further Discussion

Chapter 1   **Introduction**

1. Is ethics about being good or being happy or just being? Does ethics presume that the good life is the only path to happiness?

2. Why is it that political or religious idealism often produces greater unethical behavior than cynicism?

3. Conscience comes from a Latin root meaning "with knowledge." Does our conscience immediately and intuitively know right from wrong "when it sees it" or does conscience reflectively apply a conceptual framework to ethical dilemmas?

4. Does flattery work? If so, when is it ethical?

5. Who do you agree with more, Dilbert or Aristotle?

Chapter 2   **The First Myth of the Market: Freedom**

1. Everyone agrees that "productivity" is a good thing. Who is more productive, the engineers who designed the packaging for pet rocks or the lawyers who successfully argued the school desegregation cases?

2. If markets are dependent on regulation for their existence, how do you account for black markets?

3. If all markets are inherently regulated, what criteria would you establish to distinguish "good" regulation from "bad" regulation?

4. A legal distinction is often drawn between "positive" rights or entitlements *to* something (e.g. adequate health care, education, a minimum wage) and negative rights or liberties *from* interference (e.g. freedom of speech, freedom of religion, right to bear arms). Assuming this distinction, is a starving man's right to walk into a grocery and eat a head of lettuce (without government intervention/arrest) a positive or negative right? When local government provides a police escort at taxpayer expense for a Ku Klux Klan rally on Main Street, is this right to free speech an entitlement or a liberty?

5. Assuming that the notion of the free market is a myth, is it a beneficial myth because it promotes initiative and encourages people to take risks? Or is it a harmful myth? For example, how do we remain globally competitive while the Japanese Ministry of Trade is carefully planning with business leaders on how to corner a new high tech market?

Chapter 3   The Second Myth of the Market: Competition

1. Are men more competitive than women? Are their predominant styles of competition different? What risks does a person take in using competitive styles that are predominantly those of the opposite gender?

2. In your experience, does benchmarking produce conformity or innovation? Is the imitation of perceived winners a substitute for risk-taking?

3. How is the right to inherit one's parents' wealth ethically different from welfare? Why would one subsidy breed more idleness and corruption than another?

4. During the Great Depression, if everyone had left their money in the bank, there would not have been a run on the banks. But you would have been a fool to leave your money in the bank for this reason. Relate this scenario to the Prisoner's Dilemma. Discuss other examples of the "Prisoner's Dilemma" that you have encountered in the business world.

5. Is efficiency value-free or value-laden? Is it generally the case that improvements in efficiency create winners and losers?

6. Thought Experiment: You are the manager of a small assembly line. There are rumors of a plant shut down and you have important quotas that must be met. You encourage your subordinates to compete with their peers, awarding bonuses and praise for the fastest workers. Does it affect your strategy if the competition among the workers begins to divide along racial lines?

Chapter 4   The Secret of the Market: Borrowed Desire

1. Which archetype fits you best: consumer, miser, or gambler? Does it depend on the context?

2. Relate the Peter Principle to the Management Complex.

3. Consider the following two scenarios. A. An imitator has certain desires but is uncertain how to satisfy them. B. An imitator is uncertain what to desire. Which one of these two scenarios comes closer to explaining the theory of borrowed desire?

4. The United States is the richest society in the history of the world. Does an increase in the "standard of living" aggravate or lessen borrowed desire?

5. As people gain equality with each other in modern society, does this equality aggravate or lessen envy (borrowed desire)?

6. Is the imitator totally passive in relationship to the desires of other people? If yes, how do you account for the fact that the imitator selects some models to imitate to the exclusion of other models? If no, what motivates the selection of one model over another model? Does desire precede imitation or imitation precede desire?

Chapter 5   **The Secret of Management: Blame**

1. St. Augustine once said that "the abuse of authority is better than no authority at all." How does this statement relate to the collapse of the former Soviet bloc? How does this statement relate to the Management Complex?

2. Provide an example of the blame game in your own experience that is analogous to the story of Adam and Eve.

3. If the "Fall" is caused by the mediation of desire, does it follow that "immediate" desire is innocent? What is the difference between immediate desire and ascetic detachment?

4. Thought Experiment: You are visiting an area of racial strife, and during your visit an interracial rape occurs. Race riots result from this crime. You were near the crime when it was committed such that your testimony would bring about the conviction of a particular man (who happens to be innocent). You know that a quick arrest will stop the violence and riots. What do you do?

5. The Supreme Court has often described the right to free speech as a kind of safety valve for diffusing rebellious impulses among the populace. Rather than repressing those voices, should society sacrifice a small amount of civil peace for the greater good? Even in the case of pornography? Do punitive damages awarded by juries against large corporations also serve an important function as a sacrificial safety valve? Why or why not?

Chapter 6   **The Currency of Blame and Credit: Gossip**

1. Is office politics always a drag on productivity?

2. Groucho Marx said: "I never want to be a member of a club that would have me for a member!" How do you solve the following romantic dilemma? Among two potential lovers, whoever speaks first and reveals their attraction to the other risks being perceived as less desirable by the other.

3. If the more removed from its original source a rumor is, the more powerful it becomes, then how do you account for the "post office" effect where information is garbled and weakened as it passes from one person to another?

4. Should managers ever use gossip as a channel to carry messages to employees? Should a manager be held responsible for the "grapevine" in his or her department?

5. Do men or women gossip more? Do they have different styles of gossip?

6. In repeated surveys that list things people are afraid of, research shows that people's *greatest* fear is speaking in front of a group. This fear is greater than the fear of death, illness, snakes, bankruptcy, etc. Does this fact reflect an instinctive fear of mob behavior?

Chapter 7   The Ethics of Survival: The Boss and the Mob

1. Discuss the strategy of survival.

2. Ambrose Bierce once said: "Success is the one unpardonable sin against one's fellows." How does this statement apply to your workplace?

3. In the parable of the unjust steward (Luke 16:1-8), the rich man has a steward who is squandering his resources. When the steward is called on the carpet the steward is in a quandary because he is too weak to do manual labor and too proud to beg. In order to make friends for himself after he is fired, he calls on all his master's debtors and cancels a percentage of their debts. When the master finds out what happened he commends the steward for acting prudently.

   Consider the following interpretation: The boss's debtors had no great love for him. When the steward publicly squandered his wealth, this made the boss look bad. When the steward cancelled their debts (a small sacrifice), he restored order and made the boss look good again. The boss not only approved the steward's resourcefulness, but his good PR campaign. How different is this situation from a congressman promising tax cuts in order to be reelected? Discuss this and alternative interpretations.

4. Thought Experiment: You land a new job and bargain hard for the salary you wanted. Your employer gives you what you want which is five thousand dollars a year more than you had been making. Later you discover that a fellow employee with similar responsibilities makes more than you do. Is it ethical for you to complain to your boss?

5. How do you reconcile the survival strategy of not attracting the attention of the mob with the responsibility to challenge unethical behavior in the workplace?

Chapter 8   The Ethics of Success: Competitors

1. What are the three myths of success?

2. Discuss the myth of ingenuity. Which strategy do you think is more successful, imitation or innovation?

3. What is the relation of hard work to success in your experience?

4. Entrepreneur means "to take between." Are middle-men productive? Or are they parasitic? Do they only benefit from the ideas of the pioneers or help promote those ideas? Is selling a productive activity?

5. Is managerial work more self-expressive than secretarial work? Does the relative pay that each of the two receives make a difference? Is Michelangelo's painting of the Sistine Chapel more self-expressive than Tom Sawyer's friends' painting Aunt Polly's fence? Why?

6. Does borrowed desire always build weakness or can it help you set your goals?

Chapter 9   The Ethics of Service: Customers

1. Discuss the strategy of service.

2. Customer service always costs the consumer. Is it more ethical to package customer service as a separate charge (e.g. initial sales charge in a mutual fund) or include it as a standard element in product mark-up (annual management fees in a no-load mutual fund)?

3. Thought Experiment: You are a secretary and a single mother. You have a secure position and a potential for a raise. Something adverse occurs in the office that is no one's fault in particular. It is easy for you to pin the blame on a fellow employee who is currently on probation. Can volunteering to take the blame for this unfortunate incident increase your chances of getting the raise?

4. Is success a prerequisite to service?

5. Is survival consistent with service? Must you be detached from your own survival in order to serve others? Or do you have an ethical obligation to survive and live to serve another day? Or is this last question just a rationalization?

Chapter 10   The Wisdom of Tradition: Work

1. What is your primary mode at work: survival, success, or service?

2. Why is it harder for a rich man to enter the kingdom of heaven than for a camel to pass through the eye of a needle?

3. Distinguish between the different interpretations of asceticism mentioned in this book:

    a. the asceticism of the miser or of the Protestant Work ethic (chapter one and chapter four)
    b. the asceticism of the coquette (chapter four and eight)
    c. asceticism as punishment (chapter ten)
    d. asceticism as therapy (chapter ten)

4. What does it mean: "before enlightenment, chopping wood and hauling water; after enlightenment, chopping wood and hauling water"?

5. Is ethics about being good or being happy or just being? Does ethics presume that the good life is the only path to happiness?

Bibliography

Adams, Scott. *The Dilbert Principle.* New York: Harper Business, 1996.

Agnew, Mary Barbara. "A Transformation of Sacrifice: An Application of René Girard's Theory of Culture and Religion," *Worship* 61, no. 6 (November 1987).

Aristotle. *Nicomachean Ethics.* Cambridge, Mass.: Harvard University Press, 1947. Loeb Classical Library edition.

Bailie, Gil. *Violence Unveiled: Humanity at the Crossroads.* New York: Crossroad Publishing Co., 1995.

Bateson, Gregory. "Towards a Theory of Schizophrenia," in *Steps to an Ecology of Mind.* New York: Ballantine Books, 1972.

Campbell, Joseph. *The Power of Myth.* New York: Doubleday, 1988.

Cialdini, Robert. *Influence: The Psychology of Persuasion.* New York: Quill, 1993.

Covey, Stephen. *The Seven Habits of Highly Effective People: Restoring the Character Ethic.* New York: Simon & Schuster, 1989.

Davidow, William, and Bro Uttal. *Total Customer Service.* New York: Harper and Row, 1989.

Deal, Terrence E., and Allen A. Kennedy. *Corporate Cultures: The Rites and Rituals of Corporate Life.* Reading, Mass.: Addison-Wesley, 1982.

Downey, Michael, ed. *The New Dictionary of Catholic Spirituality.* Collegeville: The Liturgical Press, 1993.

Drucker, Peter F. *Managing for Results.* New York: Harper & Row, 1964.

_____. *Managing the Non-Profit Organization: Principles and Practices.* New York: Harper Collins, 1990.

_____. *Adventures of a Bystander.* New York: Harper Collins, 1991.

_____. *Post-Capitalist Society.* New York: Harper Business, 1993.

Durkheim, Emile. *The Elementary Forms of the Religious Life.* New York: Collier Books, 1961.

Eder, Donna and Janey Lynne Enke. "The Structure of Gossip," *American Sociological Review* 56 (August 1991).

Eliade, Mircea, ed. *The Encyclopedia of Religion,* vol. 12. New York: Macmillan, 1987.

Evans-Pritchard, E. E. *Theories of Primitive Religion.* New York: Oxford University Press, 1965.

Fallows, James. "How the World Works," *Atlantic Monthly* (December 1993).

Freud, Sigmund. "The Ego and the Id," in the *Standard Edition of the Complete Psychological Works,* vol. 19. London: Hogarth Press, 1961.

_____. "Totem and Taboo," in the *Standard Edition of the Complete Psychological Works,* vol. 13. London: Hogarth Press, 1961.

Friedman, Milton and Rose. *Free to Choose.* New York: Harcourt Brace Jovanovich, 1980.

Gates, Bill. *The Road Ahead.* New York: Penguin Books, 1995.

Gini, Al. "Meaningful Work and the Rights of the Worker: A Commentary on *Rerum Novarum* and *Laborem Exercens,*" *Thought* 66 (September 1992).

Girard, René. *Deceit, Desire, and the Novel.* Baltimore: Johns Hopkins University Press, 1965. Cited in Notes as DDN.

_____. *Violence and the Sacred.* Baltimore: Johns Hopkins University Press, 1977. Cited in Notes as VS.

_____. *The Scapegoat.* Baltimore: Johns Hopkins University Press, 1986.

_____. *Things Hidden Since the Foundation of the World.* Stanford, Calif.: Stanford University Press, 1987. Cited in Notes as THFW.

_____. *A Theater of Envy: William Shakespeare.* New York: Oxford University Press, 1991.

Greenleaf, Robert K. *Servant Leadership: A Journey Into the Nature of Legitimate Power and Greatness.* New York: Paulist Press, 1977.

Grote, Jim. "René Girard's Theory of Violence: An Introduction," *Research in Philosophy and Technology,* vol. 12 (1992).

_____. "The Imitation of Christ as Double-Bind: Towards a Girardian Spirituality," *Cistercian Studies* 29, no. 4 (1994).

Halbertal, Moshe, and Avishai Margalit. *Idolatry*. Cambridge, Mass.: Harvard University Press, 1992.

Haughey, John C. *Converting 9 to 5: A Spirituality of Daily Work*. New York: Crossroad, 1989.

Heilbroner, Robert, and Lester Thurow. *Economics Explained*. New York: Simon and Schuster, 1994.

Iacocca, Lee. *Iacocca: An Autobiography*. New York: Bantam Books, 1984.

Jackall, Robert. *Moral Mazes: The World of Corporate Managers*. New York: Oxford University Press, 1988.

John Paul II, Pope. "Laborem Exercens," *Origins* 11, no. 15 (September 24, 1981).

Kropotkin, Peter. *Mutual Aid: A Factor of Evolution*. Boston: Extending Horizons Books, nd.

Lapham, Lewis. *Money and Class in America: Notes and Observations on Our Civil Religion*. New York: Weidenfeld & Nicolson, 1988.

Lewis, Michael. *Liar's Poker: Rising Through the Wreckage on Wall Street*. New York: W. W. Norton & Co., 1989.

_____. *The Money Culture*. New York: W. W. Norton, 1991.

_____. "Republican Socialism," *The New York Times Magazine* (November 26, 1995).

Livingston, Paisley. *Models of Desire: René Girard and Psychology of Mimesis*. Baltimore: Johns Hopkins University Press, 1992.

Lynch, Peter. *One Up on Wall Street*. New York: Penguin Books, 1989.

_____. *Beating the Street*. New York: Simon and Schuster, 1993.

Malkiel, Burton. *A Random Walk Down Wall Street*. New York: W. W. Norton, 1985.

Marx, Karl. *Economic and Philosophic Manuscripts of 1844*. Moscow: Progress Publishers, 1974.

Moore, James. *The Death of Competition: Leadership & Strategy in the Age of Business Ecosystems*. New York: Harper Business, 1996.

National Conference of Catholic Bishops. *Economic Justice for All: Pastoral Letter on Catholic Social Teaching and the U.S. Economy*. Washington D.C.: United States Catholic Conference, 1986.

Orléan, André. "Money and Mimetic Speculation," pp. 101–12 in Paul Dumouchel, ed.'s *Violence and Truth: On the Work of René Girard.* Stanford, Calif.: Stanford University Press, 1988.

Oughourlian, Jean-Michel. *The Puppet of Desire.* Stanford, Calif.: Stanford University Press, 1991.

Peter, Laurence J. and Raymond Hull. *The Peter Principle: Why Things Always Go Wrong.* New York: William Morrow, 1969.

Ronsvalle, John and Sylvia. *The Poor Have Faces: Loving Your Neighbor in the 21st Century.* Grand Rapids, Mich.: Baker Book House, 1991.

Samuelson, Robert J. "The Death of Management," *Newsweek* (May 10, 1993).

Sartre, Jean-Paul. *Existentialism and Human Emotions.* New York: Philosophical Library, 1957.

Schnaars, Steven. *Managing Imitation Strategies: How Later Entrants Seize Markets from Pioneers.* New York: Free Press, 1994.

Schoeck, Helmut. *Envy: A Theory of Social Behavior.* New York: Harcourt Brace Jovanovich, 1969.

Smith, Hedrick. *The Power Game: How Washington Works.* London: William Collins, 1988.

Solomon, Robert C. *Ethics and Excellence: Cooperation and Integrity in Business.* New York: Oxford University Press, 1992.

_____. *Above the Bottom Line: An Introduction to Business Ethics,* 2nd edition. New York: Harcourt Brace Jovanovich, 1994.

Soros, George. *The Alchemy of Finance: Reading the Mind of the Market.* New York: Wiley & Sons, 1987.

_____. "The Capitalist Threat," *Atlantic Monthly* 279, no. 2 (February 1997).

Spendolini, Michael. *The Benchmarking Book.* New York: Amacom, 1992.

Strauss, Leo. *Persecution and the Art of Writing.* Glencoe, Ill.: Free Press, 1952.

Thomas, Jerry. "Why Advertising Works," *Business First* (September 9, 1996).

Thomas, Lewis. *The Fragile Species.* New York: Charles Scribner's Sons, 1992.

Thomas Aquinas, *Summa Theologica.* New York: Benziger Brothers, 1947.

Townsend, Robert. *Up the Organization.* New York: Alfred Knopf, 1970.

Weber, Max. *The Protestant Ethic and the Spirit of Capitalism.* New York: Charles Scribner's Sons, 1958.

Williams, James G., ed. *The Girard Reader.* New York: Crossroad, 1996.

Note to Reader

The authors welcome comments and questions regarding any aspect of this book, including your stories of office politics or your favorite office FAXES. Please direct correspondence to N. V. Management, P.O. Box 5546, Louisville, KY 40255 or by e-mail to NVMGMT@AOL.COM. With sufficient advance notice, the authors are available for seminars.